Cover - Coins List:

1. Costa Rica - 1935 - 1 Colon
2. Danish West Indies 5 Bit - 1 Cent - 1905
3. US - 1828 - Liberty Large Cent
4. Guatemala - 2 Real - 1898
5. Russia - 2 Kopek - 1910
6. France 10 Centimes - 1921
7. US - 1853 - Liberty Large Cent
8. Canada - 1 large Cent - 1908
9. Brazil - 200 Reis -1871
10. Germany - 5 Pfennigs - 1924
11. China Qing Dynasty Qian Long Tong Bao 1736
12. Norway - 1/2 Skilling - 1841
13. Hong Kong - Queen Victoria Dollar - 1866
14. Cuba - 5 Centavos - 1915
15. Belgium - 5 Centimes - 1929
16. Germany - 5 Pfennig - 1820
17. Peru - 1 Sol - 1884
18. Italy - 5 Lira - 1872
19. México - 50 Centavos - 1906
20. Costa Rica - 5 Centimos - 1947
21. Spain - 10 Centimos - 1850
22. Italy 10 Centisimo - 1894
23. UK - one Penny - 1928
24. Germany 1 Reichmark - 1933
25. Denmark - 2 Ore - 1927
26. Switzerland -2 Rapper - 1893
27. Panama - 1 silver Quarto - 1955

Also by This Author

Global Pension Crisis: Unfunded Liabilities and How We Can Fill the Gap
Richard A. Marin

Foreword by Robert H. Frank, *The Darwin Economy*
John Wiley & Sons, 2013

Mater Gladiatrix

RICHARD A. MARIN

ISBN: 978-1-4834-7215-7 (sc)
ISBN: 978-1-4834-7217-1 (hc)
ISBN: 978-1-4834-7216-4 (e)

Library of Congress Control Number: 2017910801

Lulu Publishing Services rev. date: 7/12/2017

I have no choice but to dedicate this book to my mother. She raised me single-handedly, and whatever I am today is largely a function of her influences on me. She was much more than a "working mother" as we know the term today. She is truly a woman of the world and the sort of rare trendsetter who changes the world without design or, perhaps, intent. To make full use of my years of Latin training and to paraphrase Theophile Gautier and MGM, she epitomized "Vitam Gratia Vitam" (life for life's sake). Her gender did not hold her back, and it would be fair to say it was irrelevant to her. She lived her life gender neutral or, more precisely, gender extraneous. I consider her *Mater Gladiatrix.*

I would also like to acknowledge Gary Reichard—a fellow Cornellian, neighbor, and provost of the College of Staten Island. Gary has encouraged me to write this story and has generously copyedited every page for me.

My wife, Kim, has patiently listened to each chapter rather than getting extra sleep. And my sisters, Kathy and Barbara—who lived every day and more of this—have indulged me this stylized and biased recounting.

CONTENTS

PREFACE

Millie the Riveter

In 1946, while Rosie the Riveter was taking her shop apron off and setting down her wrench for the last time, Millie Uher, who had just learned Spanish in an intensive language program at 30 Rockefeller Center, got in a US Army surplus Jeep and drove up into the hills southwest of Maracaibo, Venezuela. Millie had a degree in home economics from the most notable and first American coed university and arguably the premier development-focused institution in the world: Cornell University. She had nine years of experience working for the New York State Welfare Department, helping the needy in rural upstate New York who had lived through the Great Depression and then the shortages of the World War II economy.

She then heard about the work of the Rockefeller Foundation, headed by Nelson Rockefeller, the eldest son of John D. Rockefeller, the billionaire oilman who had grown up in Richford, New York, fifteen miles away from where Millie and her immigrant family had lived for the past half century. This was not about welfare. She had never been out of the United States, or for that matter, the Northeast. This was not about exotic travel. Like everything she had done in her life, she impulsively set her sights, put her head down, and got where she wanted to go … with little or no thought about where it would all lead.

Millie Uher may not be recognized as one of the greatest women of the twentieth century. She lacks the profile of Eleanor Roosevelt, Gloria Steinem, Mother Teresa, Hilary Clinton, Margaret Thatcher, or Angela Merkel, yet I believe she may have invented the modern woman and broken gender barriers before anyone knew to apply labels. And she did it with complete oblivion to any cause or mission. She did it because it was what she wanted to do and with no greater vision.

She was unaffected by the roaring twenties, skipped through the Great Depression, played golf and skied through the War, and was "leaning in" to the entire world long before Sheryl Sandberg was even born. I tend to hyperbolize when it comes to my mother. I can certainly be accused of exaggerating her impact on the world, but I will let you be the judge after you have heard her story. From immigrant's child to global diplomat. From rural schoolchild to urbane single mother. From first-generation high school graduate to PhD. From traditional American girl to emerging market adventurer before the market was thought to have any emerging in it. It is the story of the twentieth-century American woman in ascendancy and transition.

My mother was always swimming against the stream. In other words, she is a person who leads an unconventional life. It is harder and harder to lead an unconventional life. When I asked her once why she made such a bold move as to relocate to Venezuela in 1946, she paused, glanced around, and finally said, "I guess you're old enough to know." Note to self, if you ever want to get the total rapt attention of your child (regardless of age), use this line. What she explained was a speedy decision and departure from the country to avoid further pursing a torrid affair with a married man.

My shock produced a comment that has forged the base of my image of my mother. I said, "So you basically joined the Foreign Legion?" Yes, my mother liked swimming against the stream.

All during my upbringing, one of the Bohemian artifacts that always found its way to some wall—usually on a hallway wall outside the bathroom—was a small framed poem that looked like the sort of thing one finds in a dusty attic or basement box. It showed a sleepy angler drifting in his boat on a summer day with the poem below:

> Most any old fish can drift along and dream, but it takes
> a regular live one to swim against the stream.

When I researched this poem, I learned that the head of neurology at the Mayo Clinic had this same poem hanging over his desk. Apparently, it was a rallying cry to high-achieving college students who survived the Great Depression. When I would read it repeatedly while waiting in the hall for my sisters to get out of the bathroom, I would admire the sentiment. I did not even know what stream they were talking about, but it made me ready to swim against it.

What exactly is good about swimming against the stream? Perhaps the puritan ethic demands it. On the other hand, is it the contrarian nature we all swear will make us wealthy as Joe Kennedy? Maybe it is the primordial drive for the ancestral headwaters of the Columbia River where we all are drawn to spawn and die. The American dream is simply not available to those who drift along and dream—or at least not to women of the twentieth century who don't swim hard against the stream.

CHAPTER 1

Back to the Salt Mines
(Malzenice to Myers, 1892–1922)

The Uher Family in 1919 (with Josephine)

John Uher, even at age forty-five, had the look of an old and hardened soul. He sat in his bentwood, cane-seated chair, balanced on the two back legs and yet sturdied by being jammed between the old wood stove in his kitchen and the window that looked out onto Myers Road. This was his spot. Since his dear wife, Catherine, had died of tuberculosis a few months ago, his life consisted of rising early, working a full day, sitting in his kitchen chair, and watching the world go by. His work involved some combination of his gas station (two hundred yards up the road), his roadhouse (across Lansingville Road from the gas station), and his fields (he had a complete farm, but he never cultivated it beyond the vegetable garden and a few acres of beans). He cooked his daily fare of hot dogs and spinach from that chair and drank his four-to-six Carling Black Label beers, which he opened with a Coke bottle opener conveniently affixed

1

to the windowsill. He shaved his stiff and bristly beard every third day (stylishly rugged before his time) and went to Mass every once in a while at All Saints Catholic Church (also two hundred feet up the road on the left-hand side).

It was not an accident that the church was so close. John had practically donated the land for the church long before the concept of tax deductions came into vogue. He had done it for Catherine, and he was privately glad to have given her that solace to lean on in her final, painful days.

"Ludmilla, bring your father another Carling," he bellowed into the dusty house. He kept at least two cases (all returnable crates and brown, well-worn, thick glass bottles conveniently part of the roadhouse official inventory) in his stone basement where the ambient temperature never varied much from the fifty-four degrees of any good root cellar. That cluttered basement was filled with John's tools, stacks of crated bottles, and strange brewing tanks and flasks—not to mention several feral cats and (depending on the season) their latest litter of kittens. It was gradually taking on the look of the man now that the woman of the house was sixteen and was distracted by being the star guard of the Lansing High School girls' basketball team.

"Dad, I told you everyone calls me Millie, not Ludmilla," the spry, young five-foot-four point guard said as she skipped down the stairs and pivoted around the banister, practically vaulting through the dining room and into the kitchen. "Why don't we get a Frigidaire like everyone else and then you ... or should I say *I* ... won't have to keep fetching your beer from that nasty basement?"

John had sired seven children with Catherine and raised six (Pauline died, like so many children of the day, at six months) until little Josephine was tragically washed away and drowned one spring day in 1922 at the age of eight while trying to cross Salmon Creek. Now there was only Ludmilla and young Paul at home, the older siblings having all left home.

Ludmilla (decidedly not Millie to John) was the apple of his eye and always had been. Where her older sister Aggie was very buttoned up and serious, Ludmilla was a free spirit. She was a hardworking and bright student and an accomplished athlete. She dreamed and spoke of things that John did not always understand, but she did it in a way that captivated him and anyone else in the room. Whenever someone suggested doing something new and different, the first one to sign up was Ludmilla. When her cousin Betty asked her to learn tennis with her, it was a foregone conclusion that she would do so. Though tennis was a country club sport to be played on manicured lawns at Forrest Hills or smooth clay at the Cornell Cascadilla Gorge courts, it never occurred to Millie to feel excluded from its membership ranks.

When she brought her father his Carling, she did what she always did: she popped the cap on the windowsill (not bothering to use the opener), took a long swig, and handed her father the bottle. It would become her lifelong drink of choice. The bottle cap simply rolled under his chair and joined a week's supply that would be swept up on Sunday afternoon. He feigned shock that she would drink beer at her young age, but was secretly pleased that she had so much moxie.

"Dad, I want to talk to you about something," she said more seriously than he was expecting.

John was genuinely scared. Ludmilla was rarely serious with him and never asked him for anything. If she needed money, she found a way to earn it. If she needed womanly advice since her mother had become ill and died, she found it from schoolteachers or family friends. She was never a burden to John and was as independent as the feral cats in the basement. John set his chair on all fours, expecting the worst, as any good Eastern European would do.

"I plan to go to Cornell after I graduate. Aggie says I can live with her, and I already applied and got into the Home Economics School with a partial scholarship, and I'm waiting to hear from the Anthropology Department. I can work in Ithaca and earn the rest of the tuition and money for my books. It will not cost you anything—I promise. Mom knew all about it and even gave me some money she had from some insurance policy."

This was so far from anything John had expected or understood that he was truly caught flat-footed. He remembered Catherine's last words to him: "Help Ludmilla and Paul become more than we were. I have already started that." He had never understood what that meant. He had left school after about fourth grade and worked with the dogged determination to leave Malzenice (a Czechoslovakian town just northeast of Bratislava) and go to America. While he shuffled through the line at Ellis Island, the stereotypical occurred. The Irish- American immigration officer (himself probably a well-established first-generation American) changed John's last name from Uhrovcik to Uher. The drive to come to America consumed half of his quota of gumption, and the rest would be used to find his way out of the Cayuga Rock Salt mines off Lake Cayuga with the help of the Volstead Act. But more on that later.

"Ludmilla, I am not your mother, and I do not agree with this idea. Why for you want to study more? You are smart enough and pretty. I see the boys look at you. Why don't you get a job or help me run the businesses? Then, when you meet a nice boy, you can marry like your sister Agnes will," John said with a painful and purposeful expression. He loved and respected his daughter, but he was so deeply rooted in the Old World that he knew and had never left behind. He did not know what else to say.

John was born in 1887 to a hardworking, but dirt-poor farming couple in Malzenice, Czechoslovakia, the artificially merged country where the haves were generally Czech and the drones were all Slavic. John was a smart boy who instinctively knew that his younger brother Joseph was right when he whispered at night in their loft room with the hay-filled "mattress" that they needed to leave Malzenice. While the gay nineties roared on in parts of the world, in places like Bratislava, the life of local farmers was as depressed as any time anyone could remember. People today generally know about the Irish potato famine, but few are aware that the same sort of blight devastated Slovakia and neighboring Slovenia in the late nineteenth century. The Czechs saw this as the problem of their poor country cousins and not something to take the edge off the good times to be had in lovely Prague.

John and Joseph were the casualties of these hard times. Their father had gone from being a hardened farmer to a bitter and abusive father and husband. Their mother was a kind woman who knew nothing but to stand quietly by her husband no matter what. John made the call, and Joseph never blinked. Even at eleven years old, John was, in a word, shrewd. He was like Jamie in the prison camp in Steven Spielberg's *Empire of the Sun*;

he knew how to scrounge with the best. If a tally had been taken (what would have been the point?), John contributed more than Joseph to their escape fund. Truth be told, Joseph was smarter than John was, but he always did what John told him. The hierarchy of family (and his brother was all the family he recognized at that stage) was one of the few traditions John clung to as his world turned upside down.

The boys made their way to Trieste, one of the most global and least bureaucratic cities in the world. Trieste had grown up as the pirate-infested Adriatic sister city to the regal and beautiful Venice. The most important feature of the city was that its history of contraband made it a primary turn-of-the-century jumping-off point to the New World for anyone with the price of passage, whether they were of age or had papers or not. Joseph and John had neither, but they did have the name and address of some older boys who had been recruited to work in America. In fact, they even had a letter from a salt company in upstate New York, offering them (in fact, their friend, but Slavic names are so similar) employment.

They could not afford the most basic of fares on the most basic of tramp steamers heading for New York. But fortunately, crew members on these ships often got waylaid in a fun town like Trieste, and finding last-minute replacements to step and fetch for-real crew members was always necessary. Joseph and John fit the bill and lived for the sixteen days of the trip like kings compared to what they were used to at home. This was no Leonardo DiCaprio voyage, but the food was better, the beds were softer, and the work was relatively light by their standards. In fact, they had no way of knowing that working their way across gave them a chance to avoid extended exposure to smallpox, typhoid, and TB that ran rampant in steerage. Little did John know at the time, but his still unknown but soon-to-be-beloved Catherine was in just such harm's way, being coughed upon inadvertently in the steerage section of another New York-bound steamer.

John was a bit sad to see the trip end. He liked having the run of the ship, and his scrounging and petty larceny left him with more money after the trip than when he began. In fact, while he would do anything for Joseph or certainly follow him anywhere, he was shrewd enough to keep his finances to himself. As much of a cliché as it seems today, Joseph and John stood on the port rail of the *Syracusa* and watched in awe as they passed through the Verrazano Narrows into New York Harbor and steamed past the Statue of Liberty in all her iconic and symbolic glory. This was the famous Gateway to America. The *Syracusa* was bringing a boatload of mostly Baltic and Eastern European refugees to the land of the free and the home of the brave. These huddled masses were not feeling particularly free yet, and they had spent most of their bravery just getting to these shores.

Unlike Vito Corleone who, per Mario Puzo, was named after his hometown and quarantined on the island for suspicion of TB, Joseph and John made it through with flying colors—thanks to the salt company letter. In fact, where Joseph gave his name as Uhrovcik, John volunteered his newly minted name as Uher, which struck him as less Old World (what did he know of Old versus New just yet), and certainly easier to spell (he was eleven years old, going on twelve, after all and saving four letters seemed like a stroke of brilliance to him). The boys had no idea where International Salt Company was, so they followed the Slavic crowd across town to Hester Street. Whatever gateway was provided by Ellis Island, the real melting pot that started to boil down immigrants into Americans started on the Lower East Side of Manhattan. Here was where the Chinese, Irish, Italians, and Germans had all come through and where the Jews, Russians, and even the Puerto Ricans and Vietnamese passed through even long after Ellis Island was shut down.

Joseph and John took up residence in a tenement room with eight other Slavic young men, sleeping in shifts, but mostly getting to know the streets of New York. It was all pretty unusual to the Uhrovcik boys. They were country mice, and when they figured out where Cayuga Lake was and saw pictures of the presumably green countryside (hard to tell in sepia), they made their plans to head north into the wilds of the Finger Lakes. One can only imagine what would have become of a spunky kid like John in the big city. But it was simply not in the cards. It turns out you could take the boy out of Malzenice, but not Malzenice out of the boy. He was on the Lower East Side long enough to add to his repertoire of slick tricks, but he was ready to leave for upstate New York within a year.

International Salt Company became Cayuga Rock Salt in 1914 and eventually became part of a division of a group of a department of the massive Cargill conglomerate of Minnesota and … the world. At the turn of the twentieth century, it was an independent local company. Geologically, the Finger Lakes are glacial lakes formed by the retraction of the last ice age as it dragged itself back north. It is hardly original to characterize those lakes as deep scratches into the bedrock created by a glacier receding north—like a hand dragging its claw through earth. The formation apparently also led to large salt caverns and deposits that were discovered as a major source of rock salt in 1878, the same time when Edison (or perhaps more accurately, a physics professor at Cornell) was inventing the electric light bulb. Amazingly, those deposits were so rich that they are still being mined to salt roads 135 years later.

The owners of International Salt Company discovered that the short and stocky Slavic and Armenian men were very well equipped to work in the shallow mines doing the backbreaking work of hauling out the salt. Unions had not found their way to the salt mines, so the economics also worked well. Both the Armenian and Slavic communities settled just north of the mines along the shores of lovely Lake Cayuga, on either side of the Salmon Creek Ravine—the Armenians to the north (Armenian Hill) and the Slavs to the south (Slavic Gulch). Life was inexpensive in this relatively remote area, and just as everywhere else in the country, ethnic groups gathered together for cultural comfort and familiarity, slightly slowing the assimilation process.

So Joseph Uhrovcik and John Uher took the Lehigh Valley Railroad from New York City to Ithaca, New York, in the summer of 1901. It was a nice day, and while they were not low on disposable cash, their inherent frugality and desire to see and enjoy the bucolic delights found them walking the six miles to the Salt Mine. It wasn't hard to find; they only needed to follow the railroad tracks along the eastern shore of the lake. The payroll foreman almost seemed to be expecting them. He was Slavic and was quick to sign up the hearty young men who spoke his mother tongue and didn't yet know the proper starting wage (thereby supplementing the payroll foreman's pockets for a few weeks). After signing away their young lives and gaining access to the company store, where they could choose to sign away the rest, they walked another mile up the lake to the small enclave at Myers Point, where a small schoolhouse and chapel augmented the cluster of homes where their countrymen lived. They found a store by the railroad tracks where rooms were available for rent. It all seemed nearly perfect to the two earnest boys.

Ludmilla knew her father's story, and she knew he was going to have a problem with her going to college. She was the first in her family to get a high school degree (Aggie had dropped out to go to "business" school), so this was breaking new ground.

She set her jaw, a look her father had come to recognize, and looked her father squarely in the eye. "Dad, I've made up my mind, and I'm going to Cornell."

"What do you want to become? Where do you want to go?" he asked with genuine interest. "I work so hard to give you a good life here. What is wrong with Myers?"

"I thought I wanted to be an anthropologist, but now, I'm not sure. I don't know what I want to do or where I want to go, I just know I want a chance to do it," Ludmilla said under her breath, but loud enough so he would hear as she headed back up to her room to prepare her valedictory speech.

John leaned back in his chair and thought about his darling Catherine. He had first seen her a year after he started working in the mine. Unlike coal miners, salt miners don't end their days with soot caking their face and nostrils. But salt miners do find their skin made raw by the constant exposure to the sodium. So, one day after work, with his skin itching to the point of distraction, John took a bus into Ithaca to find a pharmacy where he could buy some salve to quiet his screaming dermatitis.

On the bus, two seats in front of him was a young girl with long fawn-brown hair and doe eyes that melted him. He had seen her once or twice in Myers, but she lived up the hill a way. All he knew was that her name was Catherine Mikinic and her family had come to America the same year as he and Joseph had come. The Mikinics had come from the town of Binovce, just south of Malzenice. John was fifteen now and seriously looking for a wife. Catherine was fourteen and just the right age for him. It was 1903, and John had settled in nicely at the salt mine and in the local community. Like most hardworking immigrant boys of his age, his goals of a home, family and business of his own—no matter how unlikely in the Old World or how modest by the standards of the New—were firmly fixed in his sights and were his singular and meaningful purpose. If his stare had been a laser, he would have drilled a hole in Catherine's head during that bus ride. By the end of it on Aurora Street in downtown Ithaca, he had made up his mind to woo and marry Catherine.

That bus ride proved fateful in several ways. John's itchy skin got cured, but the itch just moved to his heart. Also, on his way to the hardware store on State Street, he passed a corner bar called the Chanticleer. There was a red rooster on the sign, and the message was clear that this was a place for men to gather. John was a hardened and stocky teenager (there's a reason salt mines are often viewed as the epitome of hard work), so when he walked in, he met no resistance. As a farm boy, he had been drinking beer all his life at almost every meal, but he was used to home-brewed beer. Looking around the bar, he noticed several beer bottles with the same black label and pointed to one for the bartender.

"One Carling Black Label coming up," said the friendly barkeep.

John noted the name and repeated it to himself over and over. This was his trick for the dual purpose of a mnemonic and a linguistic crutch, even though his English was progressing nicely despite the heavy Slavic accent. He struck up a conversation with the bartender, who seemed to be Greek in origin. This whole area of upstate New York was littered with one Greek town name after another, so this did not seem out of place to John. John asked if he needed any help on the weekends taking care of the bar. Like everything John did, this was part of his plan. He wanted to spend more time in town, where things were livelier. And he wanted to take on extra work to add to his accumulating savings (hidden away in an old cigar box in his room, where he kept both paper money and all the older coins he came across … he had heard that people paid extra for good old coins). He was not so omniscient as to realize that his fortune (at least by a young Slavic man's standard) would lie in the beer business.

Years later, after her father's death, Millie was rummaging through John's possessions in the house, garage, attic, cellar, and barn. She found both her high school and Cornell commencement programs among the junk. Her father had not gone to her high school graduation (still being mad at the school system). He did, however, proudly go to see Millie graduate from Cornell in 1937.

Millie found tools and boxes strewn all over the place in the garage attic with no apparent rhyme or reason. Her brother Paul wanted the house and was likely to find use for some of the junk. John had left most or all his earthly possessions to Millie, but she would later sell the property to Paul for a mortgage that would never be paid and eventually was just torn up. But something else caught her eye in the garage attic. It was an old cigar box that she recognized from the years she had seen her father stash innumerable old or interesting coins in it. It was the only possession that she took back home with her. The coins had meant something to him, but he was not inclined to sort them out, simply saving them as important connections to the past. Similarly, Millie wanted them not for their monetary value (she had no idea of their value) but as a remembrance of her father.

John was a man of the salt mine, and any success or opportunity he seized after Cayuga Rock Salt was incidental to who he was at his core. The coins were a symbol of his commercial bootstrapped success. It all provided for his family and gave him some small degree of local status, but he lived and died a mineworker. Mineworkers ate hot dogs and spinach. They drank beer. Millie collected coins and drank beer her whole life.

The Uher Family in late 1922 (without Josephine)

CHAPTER 2

The Roadhouse Years
(Route 34B, 1922–1929)

Millie and the Texaco Truck

John Uher was a man on a mission. His mission was to accumulate wealth and make a better life for his family. Notice I did not say for himself and his family. His needs were as basic as they come, but he had married the fair Catherine Mikinic in 1907 and spent his weekdays in the Cayuga Lake Salt pit and his weekend days at the Chanticleer learning the liquor and beer business. Since the Slavic neighborhood was in the gulch of Salmon Creek at the base of Myers Road, it seemed like the right place to build a house for his growing family. There was clean, flowing water, and his brother and fellow Slavic workers and a small town of sorts were nearby.

Myers Point was one of the early settlements along Cayuga Lake. The delta of the creek had made for a flat landing area for the lake ferries, and it just so happened that the train from Ithaca to Syracuse made its first stop at the Ludlowville Station. The station was the same building in which the Uher brothers first lodged, above the general store. It was a logical and normal community based on the primary transportation modes of the late nineteenth century.

As glacial lakes, the Finger Lakes have gorges cut into the bluffs all along them on either side. Salmon Creek lay innocently on the bottom of one such gorge. I say innocently because, in 1922, the first of what would be two major floods (the other in 1935) rushed down the gorge, taking out bridges and sweeping away the Uher family home and one of their girls, Josephine, age eight, two years older than Ludmilla.

The flood of 1922 came on suddenly in a place where major acts of God were a rarity. Upstate New York may experience regular snowstorms or thunderstorms, but hurricanes, tornadoes, and flash floods were not common. Salmon Creek, in this spot, was at a meteorological vortex of sorts, however. Granite cliffs cut into the hillside over millennia could turn a bad rainstorm into an instrument of violence, enraging an otherwise mild-mannered creek.

Eight-year-old Josephine liked the out of doors and nature, so when the creek started to rise that afternoon, she walked the few hundred feet to stand on the wooden bridge to watch the rush. Had the bridge been made of iron—as it would be after the flood—the story might have been different. This time, the rush turned into a surge of water suddenly compressed by the granite walls and thrust toward the old bridge, which was never built to do more than bear an occasional delivery truck over a trickling creek. Millie watched helplessly from the porch as the surge swept the tiny bridge and Josephine down toward the lake. She had no time to ponder her sister's last confused look at her as her mother grabbed Millie's hand and ran off the porch, into the rain and up the hill toward the small wooden church, which sat about seventy-five feet higher than the Uher's creek-side home. Her mother had Millie's baby brother Paul under one arm and Millie's wrist tight in the grasp of her other hand.

As Millie turned to look back for Josephine, she was shocked to see the porch they had just left ripping from the sides of their house and joining the bridge on its trip downriver. There was no sign of Josephine. That was enough to scare Millie into pumping her legs harder up the gravel road to the Catholic church next to Uncle Joe's house.

After a blurry and hectic night with men and women coming in and out of the church frantically, Millie woke on one of the wooden pews and looked out the dirty church window down toward the creek. It looked damp, but calm and much as it always did, except that the shores were scarred and littered with debris, and several houses that had been there yesterday were now simply gone. When Millie realized that her family home was among the missing, it left a strange emptiness in her young heart.

That day, Millie and Paul traipsed behind their mother as she wandered along the creek bank picking up the detritus of the Uher family's life as they had known it. The menfolk were down by the lake, walking along the shore and dredging the creek delta with grappling hooks from small boats. They were looking for the three souls, including Josephine, who had gone missing during the flood. No one felt optimistic.

The Red Cross disaster assistance crews were on site as well. The American Red Cross had existed for forty years and had spent the four years since the War to End All Wars refocusing its efforts on safety training, accident prevention, home care for the sick, and nutrition education. Relief efforts were less routine outside the wartime environment. It would not be until the great Mississippi flood in 1927 that the Red Cross would sort out how best to help domestic relief victims.

After the Salmon Creek flood, the volunteers from the Syracuse chapter acted more as disaster voyeurs than real help. The WASPs from Syracuse were a bit at a loss as to how to help these Catholic Slavic immigrants as they took most of the real relief work onto their own shoulders. So they did what they could and handed out scratchy war surplus blankets. The Uher family received one gray blanket for the seven of them, or as the Red Cross records showed, the eight of them, the records not yet reflecting the loss of sweet Josephine. The Uher family had plenty of blankets from their friends and family.

Several years later, a Red Cross representative sought out the Uher family of Myers and—working off an officious clipboard—requested the return of said blanket. Millie had answered the door that day and never forgot that unfeeling request, saying that it caused her to recognize the need for a kinder, more impactful form of relief for the needy.

After the flood, it took two days, but Millie finally saw her unshaven father grimly walking up the hill to the church carrying the covered body of Josephine. Her small body had washed ashore down near the saltworks, and he had walked the mile down with an old sheet and a heavy heart. He carried her back to the church to be prepared for burial by her mother. It was a somber day for the family, but having had two days to grapple with Josephine's presumed death, the closure was more relief than agony. They knew from Millie's accurate account that the odds were against Josephine. She now lay in the church intact, just lifeless.

For John Uher, 1922 was a galvanizing moment. Losing a child was hard. Losing your family's home was both hard and motivating. Welfare per se did not exist, and charity available from the church was slight in a hardworking community like Myers (Myers is a village enclave in the incorporated town of Lansing in Tompkins County, New York). Help from other family members sustained the Uhers in their time of need—that, and hard work from all able-bodied family members, which meant John Jr., Peter and Agnes all had to go to work to do what they could.

But John knew it was time to change things up. Since the passage of the infamous Eighteenth Amendment, known as the National Prohibition Act or the Volstead Act, John had watched and listened carefully at the Chanticleer (or more accurately, he watched in the alley behind the bar) to understand the fine points of the new laws. It was tricky because there were the somewhat vague federal laws and the more specific—but less serious—state law, the Mullan-Gage Act.

No one knew where the lines were drawn, but clearly, the manufacture, sale, and transport of alcohol were forbidden. Near beer was okay, however, and homemade distilled fruit-based alcohol was okay to an extent—even hard liquor was okay for medicinal purposes if prescribed by a doctor. Of course, nearby Canada enjoyed no prohibitions at all. Local law enforcement was more ambivalent and confused than anyone. In these circumstances, John decided with great certainty that there was money to be made in this confusion.

While the Uher family healed its wounds, they stayed at the Uhrovcik home in two back rooms and tried to gather the bits and pieces of their lives. John steeled his resolve and began running Canadian liquor from Kingston, Ontario, brewing illegal full-bodied beer (above 10 percent alcohol content) labeled as the allowable 0.5 percent, and he even distilled a fair amount of cheap fruit wine in several abandoned warehouses by the creek that had ravaged his family. John enlisted the help of his sons and his brother Joseph. He sold his products to all the local roadhouses and Ithaca eateries that were not temperance minded, managing to flout all three prohibitions of the Volstead Act on pretty much a daily basis from 1922 to 1932. What started as a necessary risk, Jean Valjean stealing bread for the family in defiance of economic hardship and tyranny, became a bit of a righteous joke in upstate New York. There was no Elliot Ness fighting off Al Capone. There were only largely immigrant communities raised on beer, wine, and liquor, wondering why all the fuss about something as natural and basic as alcohol.

John was tough enough to stand his ground, but he nonetheless stayed away from the biggest local establishments because that was where local gangsters plied their trade—and he wanted no part of commercially inspired violence. He also learned to avoid the direct notice of the Women's Temperance League, but that activist group was simply less evident in the Catholic immigrant community.

John Uher was no shrewd investor or high liver. Every penny he earned legally, illegally, or anywhere in between went into his cigar box hidden somewhere unknown to the family (but likely invisible in clear sight). When he had amassed enough, he bought a large tract of land that was deemed undesirable because it had been split in two by an eminent domain decree for Route 34B. He bought about 120 acres despite the highway cutting through it north/south and Myers Road running through it east/west. Although John did not know it intellectually, he must have intuitively understood that the nation's transportation modes and patterns were changing the gathering places and ultimately property values, especially where commercial interests were concerned.

He spruced up the old farmhouse on the southwest quadrant and moved his family into the large, rambling two-story house. There was a detached garage, an old barn, and many unplanted fields spreading in all directions. While he and Catherine had good use for some of the land for a family garden and for the barn to house some small farmyard stock like chickens and pigs, John had seen enough of the harsh and unproductive farming life in Slovakia to know that he did not want to be a real farmer. Besides, his bootlegging had made him more of a general businessperson than anything had.

John Uher in his roadhouse

John was frugal, tough, not afraid of hard work, and personable in a very basic way. With a major road running through his property, he realized that commerce was the way to go. After getting his family properly set up in the new house (far uphill from Salmon Creek, with a much more docile brook running through it), John decided to build a gas station and a roadhouse across from each other to tap the growing traffic on Route 34B. They were cash businesses, which John could understand. The roadhouse, opened as John's Joint, was right in his wheelhouse, and gasoline was in some ways a product not unlike alcohol: someone refined it and sold it to you, and all you had to do was store it and resell it. Everything else that he sold in the gas station (under the ubiquitous Texaco brand), from the oil, Coca-Cola, and candy bars, was just icing on the cake.

Since he owned the land and had paid for the buildings in cash, income from the business was simply working capital, allowing him to pay the salaries of a few local inexpensive employees (people always seemed to need steady work). With the growing drive-by clientele, it all provided adequately for the family's needs—but just at the time the younger members of the family were growing up and leaving.

Catherine had always been prone to wintertime illnesses, including influenza. She had a year-round cough that got worse in cold weather. After they lost Josephine, she started on a slow, steady decline toward a diagnosis of the dreaded tuberculosis. John and she knew long before any formal doctor's diagnosis that Catherine had picked up a bacillus that had lain latent in her for years. She was strong. Bearing seven children was difficult, but it was far easier on her than the pain of losing two of them (Josephine and the stillborn little girl who would have been her sister). As she progressed in her illness, Catherine found the walk down (or more accurately, the walk back uphill) Myers Road to the church difficult. John knew the church was looking for land for a bigger church, so in 1930, he sold the land across from the gas station and roadhouse on the northwest corner to the diocese at a bargain price.

While income tax had existed since 1913, the concept of charitable deductions was in its infancy. For immigrants, charity started and ended with the church. With this gift, Catherine could go to church by stepping out of her front door and a few steps up the street. Catherine had a year of comfort in being close to her church, and after making John promise to help Millie and Paul achieve their educational dreams, she faded quietly into the hereafter.

When the church sale became final, the Lansing town leaders saw an opportunity, sought out John, and offered to buy all of his land east of 34B for their new unified Lansing District High School (as opposed to the Lansing Town High School from which Millie would graduate). The problem was that John and Catherine's children were almost finished with school. John had no warm feelings for any form of government after his years of skirting the law with his bootlegging. He was not about to give his land away to the town as he had done for the church, and Catherine was not by his side to cajole him.

There was also the matter of his roadhouse, which was situated on the eastern side of 34B. John had never held any debt and had no need to sell the land. He chose to wait the town leaders out, knowing that they had already accumulated much of the school parcel and needed only his road frontage parcel to complete the plan. Eventually, he sold the land to the town, but he kept the roadhouse intact. The records of that sale have been lost over the years, but I suspect that the Uher capital gain was meaningful. Now Lansing had coalesced with a church, a school, a roadhouse, and a gas station at its four corners.

While John was building his businesses and selling off his unnecessary land to help form the core of the village of Lansing, Millie was growing up during the roaring twenties. As she later told her family, she felt that there was nothing "roaring" about the twenties in Lansing and very little impact of Depression in the economy of the rural community. Her recollection was that farm communities just soldiered on and never felt the highs or the lows of those years.

While one can see how muted the economic cycles can be in a college town like Ithaca, this was particularly so for the Uher family. John Uher's lifelong distrust of leverage, his lack of sophistication with investment markets and even banks, and his fervent belief in the kingdom of cash made him largely bulletproof when it came to the 1929 crash and the subsequent downward spiral. Ithaca and even Lansing suffered less than New York City, but the Uher family truly did not suffer much at any time. Their frugal lifestyle and unassuming ways left them out of the roar of the decade, and they avoided the pitfalls of the "morning after."

As a teenager, Millie grew very close to her first cousin, Betty Zader. They were kindred spirits who were both good solid farm girls, but they were equally young women with awareness of the changing world and a zest for life that intimidated men and women alike. They both joined the Lansing High School girls' basketball team with its risqué tank tops and short shorts. And Betty got it in her head that she and Millie were destined for greatness on the tennis court—a particularly bold idea since there was not one tennis court in the town at the time.

Such details were a mere speed bump to these girls with an abundance of moxie. They found a level patch of field on what is now the Lansing High School playing fields and wheelbarrowed in enough clay from God knows where and built a regulation-size clay court. Finding canvas tape, galvanized nails, and a net presented no problem for the daughters of bootleggers—although it is unfair to imply that everything the family procured in those days had touches of larceny. Many things were merely purchased at a local hardware store or some such legitimate locale, but suffice it to say that Millie and Betty were ambitious and ingenious young women who figured out how to do what suited them. They played so much tennis in the summer of 1931 that they decided to enter the New York State Women's Amateur Doubles Tennis Championship. They made it far enough through the single-elimination tournament to get noticed as serious contenders.

Meanwhile, back at the roadhouse, competition was heating up along Route 34B. Gas stations were simple faceless utilities, but roadhouses all had a special aura to them and therefore a certain clientele. Along 34B, there was Agnes's Place about halfway up the hill, which attracted primarily young rowdies who mostly drank beer … and lots of it. At the top of the hill, by the turn toward Ithaca was the grand lady, the Rogues Harbor Inn, which served meals and had rooms for overnight guests. The name would imply a rough crowd, where, in reality—and by comparison to the pure roadhouses like Agnes's and John's Joints—Rogues Harbor was quite upmarket.

Rogues Harbor was a civilized place to eat, and Betty even waited tables there on weekend nights since the tips were respectable. Alcohol was certainly available, though not technically on the menu. The owner needed either to know the customer or feel very loose for him or her to get a drink with dinner. The rooms upstairs were another matter altogether. There, you could get any vice you chose satisfied. Since Betty's mother forbade her from going upstairs, even to deliver room service, one of the boys working the shift always had to be enlisted to do the honors. This proved no problem since going upstairs to see what was going on was a goal of all the teenage boys in town.

That left John's Joint at the bottom of the hill. John was no marketer. He understood basic human needs just fine, but he was not just old school—he was more old country. A roadhouse was for grabbing a bite in the middle of or after a long day of work, serving simple food for simple people. If it had been up to John, he would have offered only frankfurters, boiled potatoes, and spinach, but Millie and Catherine had convinced him to widen the fare just a bit to include fresh ham sandwiches, ground beef patties (hamburgers had not yet come into vogue) and fried potato wedges. As for beverages, as this was a workingman's bar, it was strictly beer or liquor. There was no wine or mixed drinks (becoming known in the twenties as cocktails) since those were what women or college boys ordered.

The Joint operated for more than thirty years, but it was pretty much unchanged over that time except for the grimy patina of age and workingmen's dirt. It had a wooden floor that was well oiled and blackened. It was so slippery when wet that the sawdust put down was not put there for effect, as at the famous Palm Steakhouse in Manhattan. The corners were pretty much rounded off by all the accumulated sawdust. The bar and tables were only a slight shade lighter than the floor, and the pattern of use made it clear that the edges were for steadying oneself when rising after a full night of liquor or perhaps for bracing against an extra special punch to drive home a point of honor.

There were eleven rusty chrome stools with mostly intact red marine leatherette tops (two had some duct tape across them). There was a circular stencil and stripped screw holes where the twelfth stool had once stood. It spoke of the violence with which it was unceremoniously removed and presumably either beaten and battered into an unusable form or carried out under someone's arm as a trophy. The gap it left was a convenient spot from which the waitress tended to the half dozen tables that sported captain's chairs that had had their spindles reinforced with steel rods purchased from the hardware store. Many chairs also had rods bracing the legs, telling the story of many years of abuse from patrons leaning back to relax.

A favorite spot in the Joint was the magazine rack that stood between the jukebox and the front door. It had been fashioned by John and was a simple wooden-stepped affair with twisted wire running across each step to keep the magazines upright and in place until purchased. But these were unlike any magazines one would find at the front counter in the grocery store. These animated and illustrated magazines could be initially mistaken as comic books, but there was nothing comic about them. Few kids could get one off the rack to look since John would yell at minors to put the magazines back and go outside to play, but these magazines were magnets to young boys.

The magazines seemed vestigial of the war years, not only addressing the prurient interests of the workingmen of Lansing, but doing so by depicting scenes of jack-booted soldiers stripping the blouses off buxom blonde women who look terrified or defiant or both. Some had been hit across the face and had trickles of blood coming down their chins; others were spitting at their captors. There was one commonality: they all had large breasts with pronounced nipples straining at their brassieres.

When her friends asked Millie about the magazines, she casually laughed like someone who grew up in and around the roadhouse and had long ago discounted the shock and awe of the magazines (not to mention the language and violence of the bar). She simply told friends that some men found the magazines interesting and that it was usually the ones who could not or did not fight who bought them. I am sure that answer confused some at the time, but perhaps it became clearer with time and a bit more maturity.

The gas station was the family source of income as the number of cars on the road grew steadily and the distance between Ithaca and Aurora/ King Ferry made the Myers stop very conveniently situated to top off before heading home. But John's Joint across the street was the center of Uher family activity during the twenties and thirties. It demanded family attention with Catherine cooking when she was well enough, bartending by both John Jr. and Peter, and waitressing and cleaning by Aggie. Although John always did the heavy lifting, he expected everyone else in the family to help.

The exceptions were Millie and Paul. For some reason, common to many families, the youngest were left to play baseball or basketball rather than putting in hard time like the older boys and girls. Millie still helped, but Paul was too committed to playing baseball as a natural catcher (short and stocky with a rock-hard arm that could easily throw to second base) to contribute his labor to the cause. The Joint became a family gathering place, and whenever family (Uhrovciks, Zaders, and other loosely affiliated Slavic folk) came by, John would hold back the check—since that was what family did.

As might be imagined, this limiting, grinding routine, coupled with the natural independence that was clearly imbued in the Uher gene pool, caused the older boys to start planning their escape from Myers. John Jr. was the oldest and logically the one to leave first. In 1925, at the age of sixteen, feeling oppressed by his father, he enlisted in the navy with the help of his mother (she endorsed his enlistment papers). He wanted to see the world beyond Myers. The world was not at war at the time, so the news of his midnight departure came as a shock to John and the rest of the family. John had forgotten how he had felt back in Malzenice. He said good-bye to his mother since he doubted he would ever see her again, given her advancing TB. John and the rest of the family had to learn of his departure from the simple note he left, declaring that he had had enough of Myers, school, and the "stinking Joint" and was joining the Navy.

He never looked back, spending the next seventy-three years away from Ithaca except for a single visit home in 1963. As a chief petty officer in the navy, he was one of those useful hardened veterans as the Navy entered World War II. He served mostly on the USS *Lexington* and saw action throughout the Pacific, including off the coast of Korea during that conflict.

John served for thirty-five years and retired in 1960 to the San Diego NCO Club that was home to so many navy veterans like John. His training qualified him to get a job as a custodian for the Chula Vista Elementary School District, and he planned to spend his final working years there.

John was an enthusiastic gambler, and since shipboard craps games were no longer available, he frequented the Caliente Racetrack in Tijuana. Every week, he left after the sixth race and after putting a ten-dollar bet down on the "5/10" (the last six races). This was the long shot ... the lottery ticket. Lo and behold, in 1963, John hit the "5/10" for $63,000 in cash. He and his Bronx Bomber wife Kitty got in a new car and hit the road right after John quit his job with a flourish. They drove east to return in triumph to the old homestead of Myers. That was his moment.

Aggie was only four years older than Millie, but truth be told, she was always an old soul. As the oldest daughter in the Uher family, she took on many of its burdens after the death of their mother. She was a serious and hardworking woman who had a lighter side that only showed occasionally, but she always focused on family and simple pleasures.

When Catherine died, Aggie was already out of the house. She had finished her education at the Catherine Gibbs School of Business, where she learned the basics of typing, shorthand, and simple bookkeeping. It was enough to earn her a position as the live-in assistant to Dr. Parker, a well-known and respected female physician who lived and practiced in Ithaca.

Aggie was given the small efficiency apartment over the good doctor's garage and had a seventy-five-foot commute to the attached doctor's office. For years, she kept the books and appointments of Dr. Parker. Along the way, she met her perfect partner, a lanky British-born grocer by the name of Arthur Gegg. Arthur was perfect because he was as serious as Agnes. Together they shed their mutual insecurities and became familiarly known as Aggie and Art.

They went toe-to-toe with each other for frugality, so it wasn't long before they opened their own Gegg's Red & White Grocery on Aurora Street in Ithaca. They were fixtures on the Ithaca scene (they never had children), joining the bowling and summer municipal golf course leagues. Bowling in winter, golfing (only nine holes at a time) in summer, and working every day all year was their life. And for Millie, they were the Ithaca rock that she always returned to visit and moor herself to when in Ithaca.

Young Paul, like his sister Millie, hankered to go off to college. It was mostly about baseball, but there was some interest in higher learning … or at least in the expanded options afforded by a college degree. Neither Paul nor Millie had any interest in the gas station or the roadhouse. They had enjoyed their youth in Myers, but like all the Uher children, they had inherited some form of wanderlust from their father. The roadhouse stood more as a symbol of "hitting the road" than as a family business to anchor their lives. Strangely enough, however, both would return to the roadhouse in different ways and with significantly different objectives.

The roadhouse years were the foundational years for the Uher family. They marked the transition from immigrants to a landed and entrepreneurial family that could evolve with hopes and dreams. Some hopes were simple and involved home, hearth, and church. Other dreams involved the wide world beyond, both with and without higher education. But the roadhouse and the Volstead Act that made it all possible were the enabling vehicles for change for this spunky family. The roadhouse and the bar business permeated the family psyche and stayed with it for many following chapters of their story.

CHAPTER 3

The Bubble in the Bump in the Road
(Myers Corners, 1929–1933)

Millie and her mother, Catherine, 1931

The area around Ithaca and perhaps upstate New York overall is more immune to the economic cycle than not, but it is not the moon and was, thus, not completely unaffected by the Great Depression. When the stock market crashed in October 1929, most people did not realize how well the market recovered in the following weeks and months. But something had changed: the optimism of the 1920s was replaced by the growing pessimism of the 1930s.

The market settled into a downward drift, only to come out of its swoon once WWII began (how strange that a world war can be a market stimulus!). But such was the broad reaction of the country and the market. The microcosms of Ithaca and Myers had several things going for them that made them different. Rural areas driven by farming generally did not feel the market fluctuations to the same extent as the nation's cities. Small subsistence-based farming (though this was decidedly not the case in the Dust Bowl), salt production (always a necessity of life, but especially so as cars hit the pavement in growing numbers and needed winter traction), and mostly communities where the major employers were about higher education (Cornell, Ithaca College, Wells College) simply didn't see the economic hardships inflicted on other areas.

Ithaca lived in a bubble back then as it still does today. While the rest of the nation stumbled and struggled mightily to regain its footing, the Uhers kept on truckin' … literally. The Texaco station and roadhouse did not boom, but they never missed a beat either. While the average American family had an annual income of $2,500, John was grossing revenues of over $60,000 from the two businesses.

Cost accounting in family businesses is usually hard to come by, and the Uher family enterprises were no exception. But given John's general frugality, his liquor and beer connections, his private alcohol manufacturing, his expanded vegetable garden and small livestock that served the roadhouse needs, and the abundance of cheap family labor until it all flew the coop, he was doing much better than the average small businessman. Throughout the Depression, he continued to stuff his proceeds into that cigar box and several larger repositories in the cellar.

It might seem surprising to those not familiar with upstate New York and its extreme differences with its downstate city cousin, but this area has always simply been behind on the development curve. This isn't unusual for rural areas like Lansing, which still lag today to a certain extent. When the Great Depression hit towns like Lansing, horses were still very much in use for both farming and transportation. The 1930s was the full transitional decade from horsepower to combustion-power. This transition probably would have occurred even faster if the roaring twenties had continued to roar, but change was happening slowly nonetheless.

This was not Appalachia, but indoor plumbing was also only on the cusp. Perhaps the biggest economic trend was reflected in the number of arable acres to move from cultivation to idleness. Some of this was based on pure economic productivity, but Lansing's arrested development was more likely socioeconomic in nature since immigrants like John Uher who had run away to escape the tyranny of the farm were more inclined to move in different economic directions. Hence, the Texaco station and roadhouse.

In some ways, however, as happens in most markets, the proliferation of gas stations and roadhouses along roads like Route 34B might have hit the saturation point. The evidence of this excess is still visible today with abandoned structures littering the roadside here and there. The intersection of Route 34B and Myers Road proved a particularly good spot that suffered less than neighboring competitors by virtue of its more logical and trafficked location.

Another phenomenon was also underway that benefited the Uher businesses. Whereas many people over-leveraged their businesses in the twenties, those properties were now owned by the banks, which meant they simply sat idle for long periods of time. Buying distressed and foreclosed property was not yet an easy or common path. Some idled farms were even taken over by the federal government under FHLA loan programs in default.

Many of those farms were simply agriculturally depleted and thus were destined to lay fallow for a long time. If banks are judged to have been slow to react to disposing of seized collateral, the performance of the US government in that regard, especially with relatively unproductive farmland in upstate New York, was even worse. These practices brought a whole new measure to slow asset turnover. Meanwhile, the debt-free Uher businesses were ascending to an increasingly stronger competitive position.

Millie and the rest of the Uher clan simply carried on. They had never had much, they had known the agony of catastrophic loss of life and home, and they had learned to be wary of overspending. Now they were moving through the biggest socioeconomic wet blanket phenomenon of the century with little or no impact. That contra-cyclicality may have been more instrumental in forging Millie's psyche than she or her family ever realized.

She spent her days going to school, socializing like any teenager, helping at home with growing frequency as her mother's illness worsened, playing sports, working at the Texaco station and/or the roadhouse, and generally pursuing her dreams and ambitions without the prevailing view that the world was a challenging and unreceptive place. Catherine's encouragement, John's hard work and conservative lifestyle, her brothers' ambitions and ultimate flight, and Aggie's solid, uncomplaining and steady support all contributed to Millie's forward momentum.

It is important to consider the broader national environment that was evolving under the leadership of the newly elected Democratic administration of Franklin Delano Roosevelt and its New Deal economics. Like many towns across America, Lansing was a direct beneficiary of the New Deal programs. The most immediate (and still visible) program was the Civilian Conservation Corps (CCC).

Since this program was designed to give work to young men eighteen to twenty years old, and the work was healthy outdoor work, many of the Uher children's friends joined up and moved into one of the local camps, where they immediately launched into infrastructure projects like rebuilding paths and trails, including the building of many beautiful stone walls along the paths and trails. Local out-of-work older men with building skills (a fairly inclusive category) were hired to lead, train, and even support (as in cooking for) these young teams.

This was all good for business on several levels for the Uhers, and it was particularly impactful on Millie. She saw the immediate and direct value of the program and internalized the lessons concerning institutional and programmatic good work that this all represented. It was good for the family, good for her friends, good for the economy, good for the environment, and just plain good all around.

The CCC paid its young beneficiaries a princely thirty dollars per month, in addition to providing them with food, lodging, and uniforms. Twenty-five dollars from each paycheck was sent directly to each worker's family, so that many families became more liquid and were thus able to buy more gasoline, eat more lunches at John's café, and even buy an occasional beer at the roadhouse.

Millie saw that the work of the CCC was also adding beauty to her favorite spots, such as Taughannock Falls and Buttermilk Falls with the creation of lovely walks, trails, and stone walls. She also saw the value of the CCC whenever nature struck the region difficult blows. Such government-sponsored assistance in times of crisis provided a dramatic contrast to how bumbling the relief efforts had been in providing help to the victims of the devastating 1922 flood. She watched as the CCC—an organized, almost military-like squad—was mobilized to help with local disasters. The visible difference in effectiveness made a powerful impact on Millie, permanently affecting her worldview.

Millie later remembered, however, that her father was more focused on the efforts of the Works Progress Administration (WPA). He viewed this, the largest of the FDR New Deal agencies, as the most meaningful because it gave real work to adult men to build the real infrastructure of the county—in his view—such as improving the roads, particularly Route 34B. These otherwise unemployed or underemployed men were his main clientele, and they all needed and spent their earnings on what he had to offer.

An important context for understanding these developments is that Lansing, like most upstate New York towns, was very solidly Republican in those days. Franklin Roosevelt never carried the vote there in any of his four presidential victories. While the political powers of the area were in opposition to the New Deal programs, they were also in direct opposition to the views of John and Millie. John took his citizenship, acquired in 1906, very seriously, though he had no trouble disagreeing with or even contravening regulations or laws with which he disagreed. Therefore, Millie got a large dose of contrarian political thought compliments of her father, himself an inherently ultraconservative man, but one who knew how to see the benefits to himself and his friends and family and could acknowledge the broader sentiment of the value of public aid.

In addition to Lansing and the Uhers muscling through the hard times of the early years of the Great Depression because of the inherent advantages that a small farming town enjoyed, they benefited directly from New Deal programs. Perhaps even more valuable to Millie's evolution into a force for change was that she saw the value of efficiently organized aid and was empowered by the major direct influences in her life: her mother's devotion to the power of education and dream fulfillment and her father's open-mindedness on the value of well-intentioned collective efforts. Altogether, the Depression was a meaningful and highly impactful time for Millie—even if she may not have consciously understood that until years later.

Meanwhile, the rest of the family kept on keeping on. Peter was the one of Millie's siblings about whom the least is known by the family. This is due less to gaps in historical knowledge than to the solitary nature of the man himself. Like his other brothers and his father, Peter was short and stocky with powerful arms and a very quiet demeanor. Whether by family experience or natural inclination, he took to the bar business.

What he did not take to were his father's dictatorial Old World ways. After his mother's death in 1931, Peter left school and went to work at Agnes's Place up the road. Although it might have been the case that the younger, livelier crowd at Agnes's was more to his liking, the more likely explanation for his defection was that it was a first step in distancing himself from his father. John was secretly unhappy about this (according to Millie) since he considered working for a competitor a direct affront to him, but he carried on as though nothing had changed.

Peter continued to live at home for a little over a year, and John simply told him to put an unspecified amount of money into the kitchen grocery jar each week to pay his share of family living expenses. It surprised no one when Peter left home after a year. Unlike John, his wanderlust was confined to the Finger Lakes area and working at more and more distant roadhouses.

Eventually Peter met and married Louise, a local first-generation girl with lots of spunk. She was the daughter of a hardened farming couple from Richford and had led a tough life with a mother who was always tough on the kids and sported a dangling cigarette from her mouth for emphasis at all times over her ninety-three years. The young couple soon cobbled together enough money to start their first bar just four miles north of Myers on Route 34B.

Eventually, they saved and borrowed enough money to buy some lakefront property and built three rental cottages, which would provide Peter and Louise with the mainstay of their income for their lives. Peter's quiet way was apparently more deeply rooted in an underlying psychological depression than anyone had the ability to recognize at the time.

One particularly difficult evening in 1956, after getting some bad news from the bank on some proposed transaction, with his two young daughters Patty and Francis and Louise all at home, he chose to end his life with the pistol he always kept behind the bar. No one understood it any more than they could have anticipated it or, for that matter, have prevented it. These were not times or people who embraced or even often encountered modern therapy. "Crazy people" were incarcerated at places like Willard Asylum, up on Seneca Lake, but mildly troubled or depressive people were left alone to stumble along until they could no longer cope. Peter just kept to himself and then dealt with his demons in the only way he thought he could.

Not surprisingly, Louise proved to be a good barkeeper and landlord, and she was able to keep the businesses running. Her daughter Patty later worked in the bars, married one of the bartenders named Pete Massicci, and stayed in the business for years. Francis, after marrying a local carpenter, headed off to the Midwest. When Patty married Peter in 1954, they bought a bar in downtown Ithaca, just around the corner from the old Chanticleer. They named it Pete's.

To this day, Patty's sons, Pete and Mike, have continued to run Pete's Cayuga Bar on Cayuga Street in downtown Ithaca. Patty's two daughters, Lisa and Karen, have also remained in Ithaca—though not in the family business. The bar has kept its local flavor rather than catering to the passing trends and Ithaca's growing college population. It too is a workingman's bar with few frills.

While Millie was the first in the family to go off to college, her brother Paul went on from a successful Lansing High School baseball career (playing on the new District High School athletic fields on the land his father had once owned) to play ball for Division III Ithaca College, where he studied recreational therapy. Although he left Ithaca, he chose to stay in upstate New York most of his life and married a somewhat well-to-do young woman from Rochester named Maryanne. They had three children—Pamela, Geoff, and Steven—and as evidence of what must now be considered the family's occupational genetics, they all eventually went into the food and beverage business.

John died in 1963 under circumstance that were a bit eerie and yet somehow consistent. At the age of seventy-six, he was robust and in fine health—one of those men who would be asked by people how he stayed so healthy. He always said it was about eating spinach every day, though Popeye was unknown to him. One day, he headed off to the funeral of an old Slavic friend with his brother Joseph at the wheel. Somewhere between Myers and Ithaca, Joseph suffered a fatal heart attack and ran off the road. Joseph and John were instantly killed. The two brothers from Slovakia exited the world just as they had entered the country: together.

When John died, he left almost everything he had to Millie. Why? As best as anyone could reason and as best as Millie could explain, the boys were men who could care for themselves. Louise had three solid businesses, and Aggie was married and commercially successful. Millie was a single mom with three kids. Simply stated, he must have felt she needed it more. Paul—or Maryanne—felt otherwise and wanted the house and the Joint. Millie was going to graduate school in Wisconsin and sold it to Paul for $10,000, which she took in a note that never saw a dime of payment and was eventually torn up.

Most interestingly, after letting the Joint sit idle and then used by daughter Pam as an antique store, in the seventies, Paul and his three children decided to renovate the Joint (the gas station had long since been sold). He and his family ran it for more than twenty years as the Corner Cupboard Restaurant.

Whenever Millie would come to visit the family in Myers during those years, she went to the Corner Cupboard since the only place to visit a restaurateur family is to have dinner at their restaurant. At the Corner Cupboard, however, she was always presented with the check at the end of her meal. Wait, as they say, it gets better. On one occasion when she asked for an extra cup of coffee because she and the family were deep in conversation, Millie's niece Pam (ironically a dead ringer for her businesslike mother, Maryanne) quietly slipped the check off the table to add the extra coffee to the bill.

The Joint may have passed down in the blood of the family, but the good graces and family values of the Uher clan apparently had been diluted in some branches. Whenever Millie was asked about this, her consistent reaction was that it was a business and it was therefore okay for her relatives to charge her. The stoic response could have been from John himself. At least in this way, the apple had not fallen far from the Uher tree.

CHAPTER 4

The Way They Were
(Cornell, 1933–1937)

Millie on Beebe Lake at Cornell

Cornell University is situated on East Hill, overlooking the town of Ithaca, New York, at the southern tip of the fifty-two-mile-long Cayuga Lake. The thing most often said about Ithaca on T-shirts is that it is "Gorges," referring to the fact that the Cornell campus is bounded on either side by the four hundred-foot deep Cascadilla Gorge to the south and the 250-foot deep Fall Creek Gorge to the north. The Fall Creek Gorge waterfall is so spectacular at a 150-foot drop, that some contend that it was the setting for early Tarzan movies. In reality, it was only the site of *The Perils of Pauline* and a random scene with a streetcar running off the bridge into the gorge. The other favorite T-shirt is much deeper than either gorge, emblazoned with the message: "Ithaca: Ten Square Miles Surrounded by Reality."

The university was founded in 1865 and is special for many reasons, among them that it was one of the first dual land grant/endowed universities in the United States, one of the first coeducational universities in the United States, and one of the first nonsectarian universities in the United States. Its motto is to be "an institution where any person can find instruction in any study." It has been described as "the first truly American university" because of its founders' revolutionarily, egalitarian, and practical vision of higher education and is dedicated to its land-grant mission of outreach and public service. This made it amazingly enlightened in its early days. In fact, this tradition has been largely maintained over the years to the point where the alternative lifestyle *Utne Reader* magazine has named Ithaca the most enlightened community in America, over and over again.

In *The Way We Were*, Barbra Streisand and Robert Redford meet on a campus that screenplay writer Arthur Laurents based on his college days at Cornell. The setting closely resembles Cornell's hilltop campus with its traditional quads and its ivy-covered stone buildings. That movie begins in the tumultuous 1930s with a fair-haired athletic fraternity man, Hubble, meeting a hardworking, city-bred activist coed named Katy, who was very much unlike the sorority girls the privileged Hubble usually hung around with. The two shared a love of prose and flirted from a distance as the politics of the day (rising Fascist threats from Europe and sweeping Communist thought from Russia and that bastion of socialism, New York City) kept them safely apart. The movie bears an uncanny, but not exact, parallel to the life Millie began to lead when she matriculated at Cornell in the New York State School of Home Economics.

Leaving home for college was not the rite of passage it is today for kids and empty-nesting parents. Aggie picked up Millie in a borrowed Ford Model A, the common man's vehicle of choice in 1933. Her possessions were few and simple and the good-byes were brief. Her father feigned needing to go to the barn, hugging her good-bye, asking her to visit often, and letting the screen door slam behind him as he trudged the 120 feet down to the barn in his baggy chinos, yellow heavy cotton T-shirt, navy blue kerchief around his neck, and dirty Carling cap on his head.

Aggie and Millie unceremoniously packed the rumble seat with Millie's things and bumped their way up to 34B for the six-mile trek into Ithaca. Millie would be staying with Aggie—with Dr. Parker's permission and a promise that she would rake leaves and shovel walks in exchange. Since they had decided that their weekly food and utilities allowance would be eight dollars, Millie would have to find work to carry her weight. As sisterly as Aggie was, money and responsibility were not taken lightly. Millie knew she would be expected to do as she had agreed without exception.

Millie and sister Aggie as roommates

Nevertheless, Millie's heart was light as she bounced into Ithaca that day. Earning grocery money and making her way up the hill from downtown Ithaca to the Cornell campus were trivial issues to her. This country girl was 100 percent confident about those sorts of trials. She was more concerned about being on such a large campus with so many well-educated men and women from all over New York and the United States. She was a small-town local who lived off campus and had no idea whether college would be easy or hard to manage.

During her first week, all of those concerns faded away. It all began with the famous Cornell swim test. It was a founding rule at Cornell (as it is today) that every Cornell graduate would know how to swim. In those days, too many young people died of drowning. The college fathers were determined to eradicate that particular scourge. Millie's first college appointment was to go to the girls' gymnasium for her swim test. Except for the fact that the girls had to take the test in the nude, this was a breeze for Millie. Since her sister Josephine's drowning in 1922, all of the Uher children had learned to swim and spent countless summer hours at the lake and in various creek swimming holes, splashing back and forth.

The swim test consisted of one round-trip lap, proving that you would not drown for the several minutes required. When the whistle blew for her cohort's turn, she jumped in feetfirst as instructed and promptly and easily swam the short lap. When she looked back, she saw that she had beaten her closest competitor by half a lap. When she exited the dressing room, one of the swimming coaches asked if she wanted to join the swim team. Millie's natural instinct was to say yes, but she held back since she had no idea how much spare time she would have at college.

As she began her classes in the new Martha Van Rensselaer Hall just off the Agriculture Quad, Millie began to realize that her course work was no harder than what she had taken at Lansing High School. She had really wanted to study anthropology, but the College of Arts and Sciences never got back to her with a scholarship offer.

Her courses consisted of Introductory Biology, Nutrition (food science), Consumer Economics (topics such as "dandelions as a cash crop"), Household Management (setting and keeping a budget), and Introduction to Education. She correctly suspected that the home ec curriculum would be a bit easier for her than for "city girls," but the truth was that Millie was focused and smart. As the movie declared about Hubble, she was like the country that spawned her: things came easily to her.

While some may think home economics is about making less lumpy gravy or what setting of the iron is best for rayon, this greatly underestimates what Cornell was trying to promote with their specialized state school. While it's hard to deny that for farm girls like Millie, the school seemed more practical than studying humanities, in actuality, home economics was a far more progressive area of study. It was all about bringing a significant amount of science into the rural home. And as in Millie's case, it was as the school itself characterized it—a path for young women to enter higher education and leadership positions in public education, academia, government, and industry.

For spare cash and grocery money, she took a job at Willard Straight Hall, the student union. It was down the hill from where her classes were, but convenient in that it was closer to Collegetown, where she could catch a streetcar or bus down Seneca Street to her apartment after slinging hash to the frat boys who lived down Library (Libe) Slope in the McFadden and Baker dormitories.

Millie loved every minute of being at Cornell. She loved the independence. She loved living on her own with Aggie (she only now realized her father's house had taken on an old woodsman's air and odor). She loved working at the "Straight" and getting to interact with all the boys from Arts and Sciences and Engineering. Up the hill, the girls went to home ec while the farm boys were in the Agriculture School. She knew lots of the home ec and Aggie crowd, but she was intrigued by the frat boys in Arts and Engineering who had come to Cornell from New York, Boston, Chicago, and even Los Angeles.

Sometime during her first few weeks, Millie had been sitting on the grass on the Arts Quad on an Indian summer day, reading about food science. This was before the invention of the Frisbee, so throwing around a Spaulding rubber ball was the 1930s equivalent of that later college quad sport. On this day, a young couple was doing just that. Millie noted the smooth athleticism that both exhibited, and her stare must have been noticed. They came over and asked if she wanted to join. Having already kicked off her shoes, Millie jumped up in her bare feet, took the ball out of the man's hand, ran a hundred feet or so into the quad, spun, and threw it back to him. Her new acquaintances were duly impressed.

Most girls simply couldn't throw like that, but Millie had shagged so many tennis balls with Betty that throwing overhand was second nature to her. After the three played catch for a while, they all retreated back to where Millie had left her shoes and books and made their introductions. The strapping young man—six foot four with a dashing Clark Gable mustache—introduced himself as Irving Jenkins from New York City. The girl, who was perhaps five foot seven, was Kay Hughes from Connecticut. Millie, five foot four, said, "Millie—and I'm local." She then excused herself, explaining that she had to run to work. Irving and Kay said they were going to the Straight to eat dinner anyway.

The three became good friends, adding to their band a few more of Irving's friends from the heavyweight crew team, as well as Aggie, who— as Millie was surprised to learn—could more than hold her own with the Cornell crowd. Irving was the Hubble character in spades. Tall and muscular, Irving had been a heavyweight Golden Gloves boxing champion in New York City, where he grew up. But he was also a bit like Katy in the movie; despite having the name Irving Aaron Jenkins and a father who was a union labor organizer with an office at Union Square on the Lower

East Side (he claimed he was not Jewish), he was studying agronomy in the Agriculture School. This blend confused many.

Kay was a literature major in Arts and Sciences and a member of the Kappa Alpha sorority. She confused no one as an obvious young woman of privilege, though she chose to be less sorority-like and more free-spirited. These attributes led to her and Millie becoming best friends throughout their Cornell years and beyond. Irving was another matter altogether. He, like Millie, had a life to live … and what a life. But lives sometimes take twists and turns and even wend their way back toward each other in ways least expected.

Irving's story over the next several years is worthy of a small sidetrack. He was a true student athlete who also had a healthy amount of empathy for the common man. His upbringing as the son of a New York labor organizer gave him a decidedly socialistic bent. In fact, one might suspect that Irving was a member of the Communist Party during his college days on the hill. But as a varsity athlete, he spent much of his time at the Cornell boathouse either relentlessly training in the "erg tanks" or out on the water as one of the Boys in the Boat. In fact, the Cornell heavyweight crew boat that lost the 1936 Olympic trials to the now-famous University of Washington boat contained Irving at stroke. The book about the boys in the boat heralds the Washington crew as having "vanquished the sons of bankers and senators rowing for elite Eastern universities." Well, not all were sons of privilege. Irving was among them, and this loss on the water led him to an amazing experience.

In the year running up to the Berlin Olympics, the controversy on the US team participating in Hitler's showcase raged, as has been seen in many movies, most recently the Jesse Owens story *Race*. The less well-known story is about the formation of the Alternative Olympics Team that set out for the People's Olympiad planned for Barcelona as a protest to take the spotlight away from Berlin.

While the US Olympic Committee formally decided to go to Berlin, many students (particularly from liberal-minded schools like Cornell) chose to follow the path of the Soviet Union, announcing their decision to participate in the Barcelona alternative. Irving was one such student. As a champion Golden Gloves boxer, he easily earned a place on the alternative heavyweight boxing squad. So off to Barcelona went Irving with Kay, Aggie and Millie waving him farewell at the Ithaca station of the Lehigh Valley Railroad.

The fervently anti-fascist, Irving was a jovial, happy-go-lucky man of six foot four and 240 pounds in a world with average men of five foot eight and 150 pounds. He thoroughly enjoyed his first trip out of the country. In the warm summer days leading up to the sporting event, he sparred with other young men, but he mostly ran and exercised as the crew team regimen had trained him to do. He was one of six thousand international athletes who gathered in Spain to compete, lodging in local homes and union halls.

Adolph Hitler became annoyed, however, that this People's Olympiad was gaining traction. Since he had already forged an alliance with General Francisco Franco about the disposition of Spain in the coming European "realignment," he prevailed on Franco to adjust his plans and launch his first attack of the Spanish Civil War on Barcelona, just days before the games were to begin.

The surprise military action caused Irving and many other athletes a great deal of immediate angst. As athletes are generally free of physical fear, they defaulted to their fight instinct. As socialist sympathizers, moreover, they were appalled and rebellious. But as young adults unaccustomed to the horrors of war, they more often gravitated to the flight instinct, encouraged by the organizers and national adult supervision in presence. No one was more adamant about evacuating its athletes than the American team. In 1936, anti-fascist sentiment notwithstanding, the United States was doing its best to remain neutral in Europe's squabbles. Reluctantly and with plenty of ambivalence, Irving went with the Americans to the US warships that had intentionally moored off Palma. Several hundred athletes (mostly young women) stayed in Spain to fight with the militia, but Irving and most of the other athletes steamed back to the United States in time to start the college academic year, which would be Irving's last before graduation.

When Irving returned to Cornell that fall, he was jokingly referred to as the "Archduke," which was a thinly veiled, educated man's joking reference to his having "started" the next major European conflict. Little did his friends know how portentous that joke would be.

During his final year at Cornell, Irving asked Kay to marry him. Millie would be the maid of honor. The plan was for him to take a tramp steamer to Hawaii for a last hurrah and to save up his summer wages while Kay did likewise by working in a publishing house in New York. After training across the country to board his ship in San Francisco, Irving landed in Hilo on the Big Island of Hawaii. He had never seen such natural beauty, and as an agronomist, he was in awe of it all.

The Big Island was agricultural, and disembarking in Hilo Harbor had the air of a James Michener novel, with port activity unloading equipment and newcomers and loading agricultural goods. It was not hard to find a summer job on a pineapple plantation. With his agricultural degree, he was immediately made the manager of two thousand field workers, mostly Asian laborers, and was suddenly cast into the role of overseer.

Irving was issued a horse and a cottage on the property. In the best mercantile tradition, this meant that the saddle and the furnishings had to be purchased at the company store on credit. Irving became a *paniolo* (Hawaiian cowboy), spending his days in the shadow of Kilauea Volcano, looking out over Kealakekua Bay, and riding the pastures of Waimea. The lifestyle was soothing and pleasant for a city boy, even one who had known the bucolic pleasures of Ithaca.

Irving had planned to return to New York, but the onshore breezes and the paniolo life were too sweet. He was in heaven—and, of course, there was that debt to the company store.

One day, while Irving was riding along the beach, he noticed beautiful blue objects in the sand. The objects were glass balls that had washed ashore. They had a hand-blown look, a roughness of abrasion from the surf, and an unnatural beauty. That evening, watching the sunset and storm clouds from his veranda, he showed the globe to his houseman, who had come to Hawaii forty years before from Okinawa. The man cradled it like a precious gem and explained that it was a float from a Japanese fishing net. It symbolized home and good luck. Irving told him to keep it and was given a gracious bow.

Shortly thereafter, Irving wrote his family that he was not returning and would stay to live in Hawaii. The hardest letter he had to write was to

Kay. He figured Millie would hear of his plans from Kay. He soon after married a navy nurse and managed to pay off his debt to the company store. During World War II, he served as governor of the island for the US Interior Department. He managed the plantation from horseback for forty years. And every day, he rode the beach in search of the globes. He accumulated a collection by the time he left Hawaii and often said that his life's good fortune was in the globes, which he spent his later years giving out to all he met.

Millie's senior year came upon her with the same gravitas as for all college students. In thinking through a career choice (she was eventually granted a scholarship to study anthropology, but she was too entrenched in her studies by then to change), Millie had known for some time that she wanted to enter into social work. Teaching was not of interest to her, and business made her think of Myers Corners and was not for her either. She liked people, and she liked helping people. Social work seemed natural to her. While she was committed to the work, however, it would be inaccurate to say it was a passion. Millie was passionate about life, and there were lots of things she liked to do.

Over her four years at Cornell, she matured from a girl who liked sports and school and occasionally thought of boys to a vivacious young lady who was an avid sportswoman (she had shifted from basketball to tennis, golf, and skiing). She was a thoughtful student who cared more about the discussion than the grades and a lively social animal who dated widely. She was very popular with both guys and girls because everyone saw her as a free spirit and fun to be around. Serious in class, out of class, she was game for most anything.

Somewhere along the way, she met a few guys who were avid skiers. In the 1930s, there was little skiing in the Finger Lakes area. There was plenty of snow—but no hills to get a good run going. Even in Vermont, where skiing was taking hold in a big way in the White Mountains and Green Mountains, the typical ski area consisted of, at most, a rope tow of 1,500 feet where the rope was powered by an old truck engine up on blocks. It took a rugged guy to put up with the fledgling sport and an unusually athletic girl to even try doing it. Only young women with lots of moxie made it past a first run. Millie didn't like skiing—she *loved* skiing. To her, it was the perfect sport: outdoors, brisk, athletic, and unusual. It embodied the essence of freedom to her. The ones who skied were mostly the same guys who were talking about going up to Canada to join the RAF to be fighter pilots for the growing British air war.

During her junior year, still working at the Straight (she was now a dining room shift supervisor), she noticed a slightly older student who studied every night in the small library on the main floor. He also worked as the librarian and locked up. This was not the big Memorial Room with the banners and flags; it was the quiet little library that few students even noticed just to the left after entering. This student was also not the big flashy Clark Gable sort (like Irving), but a quiet law student of normal height and size. He and Millie often found themselves being the last to leave and lock up at night. They struck up a friendship, and while she told him things he didn't know about Cayuga Lake and the dozens of local waterfalls (many known only to the locals), he told her about skiing, which was his passion. This man was decidedly not the RAF type. Dave (not his real name) was married. In fact, he was the only married friend Millie had. His wife, a Cornell alumna herself, had been in a bad skiing accident and was laid up with a broken pelvis at her family home in New York City while Dave finished his law school curriculum. He and Millie started spending more and more time with one another, including a first ski weekend in Dave's home state, Vermont, in the spring of 1936. It was a clandestine tryst, but it was not romantic, just intimate. Dave spent the weekend teaching Millie to ski. Millie, in turn, taught Dave how to look beyond his law books to find the passion in his life. The passion they both shared was skiing and a lust for life.

Dave graduated law school with honors and the distinction of being on the law review. He left for a top-notch job in New York City, where his wife had recuperated and was decorating up a storm at their new Beekman Place co-op apartment, compliments of her parents. On that graduation day, Millie was playing a round of golf with three of her favorite RAF boys. Her focus on her golf game was usually good, but she was thinking of a snow-covered slope in Vermont and skiing with Dave.

Millie spent the summer of 1936, her last summer vacation, working back in Myers. She had taken a summer job with the New York State Department of Recreation as a camp counselor of sorts. The job was to set up and run a summer program for a gaggle of children whose parents both had to work or where there was a single-parent home. These were children who were perfectly normal except for the fact that their parents were working class and lacked the money for a private camp or the extended family to watch them at home.

Millie liked working with kids, but what she really liked about the job was the freedom to design the program. Being able to do this in Myers and stay at her father's house for a last time was a bonus. It teed her up for a more serious senior year and her vocational search. Knowing that Dave was 230 miles away in New York City also made her more serious about what lay ahead.

Most of Millie's senior year was spent on course work in economics and education. These were the studies that resonated most with her. The domestic or lifestyle courses were less interesting. On the social side, she chose to spend her time with Kay and Irving as they finished their studies and planned their lives together. Since Kay's classes were on the Arts Quad and Millie and Irving's classes were up the hill on the Ag Quad, Millie naturally saw more of him than she did Kay.

But Irving had changed since his Barcelona adventure. He was as courtly as ever, but he had a decidedly more worldly way about him. His Olympic adventure and his crew team experience made him a natural candidate for Cornell's senior honor society, Sphinx Head. The *New York Times* declared the society "the highest non-scholastic honor within reach of undergraduates," and membership in it put Irving into a select group of high achievers.

As Kay approached graduation, her eyes were on New York City with all its publishing glamour. Irving, on the other hand, having seen a bit of Europe and the world, wanted to see more of the world, including getting a taste of the Far East and Asian horticulture. For her part, Millie had a challenging blend of desires. She had already secured a job with the New York State Welfare Department, her employer of choice. Her Cornell degree and top grades gave her the unusual choice of where in the state she wanted to work. Historically, Cornellians either aspire to get far away from Ithaca or never leave.

Millie was ready to get away. That winter, she had met Dave in Vermont for skiing trips. Their friendship had moved to a new level as much because she thought it the right thing to do as for any other reason. Millie asked for assignment to Plattsburgh, a town on Lake Champlain, feeling that separation was somehow symbolically correct.

Graduation 1937 was a typically bittersweet day. Millie, Kay, and Irving walked together from the Arts Quad to Schoellkopf Field. Although they were supposed to walk with their own schools, no one policed that sort of thing too rigidly. After the ceremony, they agreed to meet at the Clinton House in downtown Ithaca for a farewell drink. There they said their good-byes and toasted their years at Cornell and "the way they were" in their student years.

CHAPTER 5

Tuckerman's Ravine
(Plattsburgh/Norwich, 1937–1945)

Millie on the headwall of Tuckerman's Ravine

Skis were a Scandinavian invention that were largely unknown to New Englanders before 1900. Swedish and Norwegian immigrants brought over a few pairs of these strange eight-to-twelve-foot wooden slats, but it was a Dartmouth carpenter by the name of Fred Garey who got a look at a pair from a Swedish student and started making them from ash wood and leather strapping to sell to students. Thus, the nexus of the sport evolved around the midpoint intersection of the states of New Hampshire and Vermont.

The manner of engagement involved carrying the skis on your shoulders up a snowy hill, strapping them on your boots, and then taking an exhilarating and somewhat hair-raising ride down the slope and around whatever obstacles (such as trees) existed on the slope. Thus, it was not a casual sport, but a rather vigorous aerobic endeavor that must have posed special challenges to even young skiers who smoked—as so many did. Those with the lung capacity were always looking for more open slopes that were climbable and presented a nice sunny southern exposure. In the area of mid-state Vermont, such a place was on the southern slope of the Grand Dame of the White Mountains, Mount Washington.

By Rocky Mountain standards, the 6,400-foot elevation of Mount Washington is not so high, but the glacial cirque that forms the south-facing ravine is as open and beautiful as any in the Western United States. This ravine, named by the naturalist Edward Tuckerman, was first skied in 1914 due to the extremely avalanche-prone nature of the cirque and the steep headwall it presents. It became clear to the National Park Service that skiers should be allowed on this slope only in late spring. This meant that the original spring break spot for the Ivy League collegiate crowd became this bowl in the White Mountains of Vermont, Tuckerman's Ravine.

Millie got her first car from Aggie. It was the same 1931 Model A that the two had borrowed to move Millie from Myers to Ithaca in 1933. (Aggie had bought it in 1935 from one of Dr. Parker's patients and had given it to Millie as a graduation present.) Millie had marginally more "stuff" than she had had in 1933, but it all still fit in the rumble seat. Millie loved driving on the winding roads of the lower Adirondacks on her way to Plattsburgh. She was doing exactly what Aggie had told her not to do, "driving like sixty"—a speed on those roads that was more like a rip-roaring forty-five. She was on her way to open the first welfare office in Plattsburgh. She would report to Dorothy, the manager who oversaw the region along Lake Champlain from her office in Glens Falls.

Plattsburgh is the seat of Clinton County, at the mouth of the Saranac River on the western shores of Lake Champlain. It was incorporated as a city in 1901, but its history predates the founding of the United States. For example, it is the venue where Benedict Arnold was defeated in 1776 in the first naval battle between the British and American navies during the American Revolution.

Those who know the Adirondacks region of New York are familiar with the juxtaposition of the raw beauty of the surrounding countryside and the rural poverty brought on by the region's remoteness and a dearth of economic opportunities. This was the exact sense Millie had when she first drove through the area in the summer of 1937. All the times she had driven to Vermont to ski over the previous two years had taken her across from Lake George (a favorite playland for New Yorkers) to Rutland, Vermont. This meant she had never driven up along the western shore of Lake Champlain. If she had, she might have seen some development for winter sports around Lake Placid due to the 1932 Winter Olympics held there. Other than those facilities, however, the area was pretty raw.

After Millie had accepted her new job, Dorothy had scouted out Plattsburgh and rented a small storefront on Brinkerhoff Street for the welfare office and a small apartment for Millie. The apartment rental was presumptuous, but it suited Millie just fine. She was all about work and life experience and placed lifestyle (as in her living quarters) very low on her list of priorities, a characteristic that would define her for years to come. As Millie pulled up to the apartment (actually just a few ground floor rooms in a local home), it reminded her of home in Ithaca.

Millie settled in quickly, a trait that would also serve her well in the years to come. She put her head down and dug into the business of overseeing government-sponsored health and human services in the greater Plattsburgh area. The social and health challenges in the area included higher-than-normal levels of teenage pregnancy, generally poor levels of family nutrition, particularly in the winter months once the vegetable gardens were out of commission, and abusive family situations where children were beaten beyond a then-generally acceptable level of parental corporal punishment.

She saw the impact of all of this firsthand with people who were not so different from her and the folks she grew up around. Seeing these hardships was particularly difficult for her since she had learned during her four years at Cornell that not everyone in the world treated their children and family badly as a normal course. She also better understood the human development impact of maltreatment on the psyche and motivation of women and children. As she tapped into state funding and programs for the benefit of her constituents, she also saw firsthand what would become a basic tenet of developmental philosophy. If you gave a man a dollar, that dollar had a 10–20 percent chance of being spent on the immediate welfare of the family, but if you gave a woman a dollar, there was close to a 100 percent chance that it would directly benefit the family.

This was actually an earthshaking, even if perhaps now obvious, realization, and Millie brought it up to Dorothy and the senior team in Glens Falls. It was surprising to none of them, but what was surprising was that Millie was questioning whether it meant that the Welfare Department needed to alter its protocols to emphasize grants directly to women rather than to men. In 1937, this was a monumental and radical suggestion. Men ruled the roost. Men made the laws. Men mostly ran the organizations like the New York State Welfare Department. And the men in the room when Millie brought up the suggestion at a regional staff meeting were appalled at the idea. Sexist bias, even in this relatively enlightened time of the New Deal, was somewhat off limits, but reverse discrimination against men was heresy.

Dorothy took Millie aside and told her that privately she was intrigued with her idea and liked it, but that the system was not ready for such radical thinking, and she should pack this idea away for a later day … perhaps in the next century. Millie was less upset than perplexed. It was the first time she had run into organizational rigidity of this magnitude, and it stopped her wildly altruistic psyche dead in its tracks.

But Millie was a farm girl who had seen a lot and been up against a lot. She was nothing if not practical, so she followed Dorothy's advice, tucked her idea away, and refocused her efforts on standardized programs and tactics outlined in the New York State Welfare handbook for extension service employees. What she really did was go on autopilot and used the oncoming early winter months to prepare herself for some serious spring skiing.

While the Dartmouth students were getting outfitted with their first ash wood skis made by Fred Garey, everyone was trying to find new and better places to ski and new and better ways to get more ski runs in versus calories expended climbing up the hill. The latent interest in skiing got a huge boost from the Winter Olympic Games in Lake Placid, and that enthusiasm easily found its way over the Vermont state line.

In 1934, the first rope tow was introduced in Woodstock, Vermont. The tow was less an invention than an adaptation since there were similar contraptions in California and Quebec, but it still reflected Yankee ingenuity. It involved a Ford Model T engine and 1,800 feet of heavy-gauge rope tied to an uphill tree via pulley. Clint Gilbert's farm in Woodstock covered a gently sloping nine hundred-vertical-foot run and was just the beginning. Soon, people all across Vermont were enlisting the CCC crews to cut trails (one of the crew's specialties) into the sides of mountains to create better and longer ski runs.

In 1939, the governor of Vermont authorized the lease of state land to a private group to form Mount Mansfield's Smuggler's Notch Area. It was the first privately run formal ski area. By the winter of 1940, the operators had constructed a one-mile aerial chair to get skiers up the hill. This was the first and biggest lift of its kind in the world, and it broadened the appeal of the sport way beyond the rugged outdoor enthusiasts and woodsmen who had dominated it to that time. No more rope burns and shredded mittens from the rope tow. No more wobbly moments while following the twin ski ruts up the hill. Now all one had to deal with was the challenge of gracefully getting on and off the chair lift and the hope that her legs had not fallen asleep on the ride up such that the dismount was somewhat less graceful.

That same year, back at nearby Mount Washington, organizers put on the third of what became known as the American Infernos, a top-to-bottom 4.2-mile race on the mountain and down through Tuckerman's Ravine. The course was modeled after the famous downhill races in Mürren, Switzerland. It was this sort of extravaganza and derring-do that really created buzz about this new sport and drew added recruits to its ranks.

Millie spent her years in Plattsburgh focused on her work and community by day and plotting and planning sporting outings by night. She played tennis and honed her golf game on the many local courses that saw very little midweek use due to the fact that they were mostly for the vacationing and weekending crowds from New York City and Albany. In the winter, it was all about skiing on rugged Tuckerman's Ravine and testing out newer ski areas such as Smuggler's Notch. She had a regular posse of young sporting enthusiasts from Plattsburgh and Vermont with whom to play, but she always looked forward most to getting a long-distance call from Dave, saying he would be free to come up and ski on one weekend or another.

Because Dave was a married man—and married to a fellow Cornellian at that—Millie always felt sheepish about the relationship. It had evolved so naturally and continued to revolve around their shared passion for skiing. Nevertheless, none of her Plattsburgh friends knew about Dave. Millie was very careful to ski where and when she knew her gang was not going. In addition, no one in Millie's family knew about Dave except for Betty Zader.

Millie was never able to share this information with Aggie because she knew she couldn't withstand the steely-eyed Catholic glare she would get from her sister. Nor could she tell Kay because the latter was still in mourning from the loss of Irving to the pineapple plantations in Hawaii. She could not tell Irving because Irving was incommunicado ... probably forever, as far as she knew. So she told Betty, because Betty was as free a spirit as Millie, and even though she had remained in the Ithaca area, Betty just seemed more worldly and accepting than most of Millie's acquaintances. Though not a churchgoer, Millie made sure always to confess her sins to a priest before rushing out to wherever she was supposed to next meet up with Dave.

As the spring of 1941 came to a close with one last trip to Tuckerman's Ravine, Millie began thinking about how she could last until the next ski season without seeing Dave. He had invited her to New York City once, but that was a long trip in those days, and while cost never seemed a deterrent to Dave, it made her uncomfortable to consider having a tryst so close to his marital home.

Millie was in no way bothered by the enforced absences. She loved Dave, but she simply had no interest in marrying anyone and was dead set against doing anything to undo his marriage. She was not a dewy-eyed girl looking to steal someone's husband. She was a fun-loving yet serious young woman who had a passion for adventure. Skiing was her adventure sport, and Dave was her copilot. On that spring trip, she asked Dave if he wanted to try a game with her. How about skiing Tuckerman's in the morning and then driving like the wind down to a small golf course near

Haverhill, where the course was open for early rounds. She positioned it as a sort of ninja challenge of the day … ski and golf in the same day. Dave loved the idea and said he was in.

As much as Millie wanted to do the ninja challenge, she really wanted to set up a warm-weather relationship with Dave that was not forced, but came naturally. So she used this manufactured challenge to get Dave to become a golfing partner as well as skiing partner. Their challenge day was a big success that Millie would repeat with Dave and with her other friends whenever she could.

Millie did not dream of golf the way she dreamed about skiing, but she had become an avid golfer nonetheless. In the 1930s, especially in northern New York, golf was less the elitist sport it seems today in urban areas where club memberships are prohibitively expensive and country club cotillions are the social scene. Rather, it was viewed more as a nice walk in the country with a few sticks and a ball. Lots of locals played, but mostly it was the young folks like Millie. She was pleased to see how much Dave also enjoyed golf, and the stage was now set for a more pleasant summer season for her.

Unfortunately, Dave and his wife had a beach club attached to the New York Athletic Club—Dave was a member—and they had a pretty busy social calendar that revolved around it. So while Millie got to see Dave for a few golfing weekends over the summer, it was only a bit better than before. In these circumstances, Millie had a choice: she could gear up her local activities and dating program or throw herself into her work. She chose the latter. The Plattsburgh area had never been taken care of quite so well as during those years when Millie's energies were diverted into overtime programming for the women and children of the neediest category in this rural yet bucolic wasteland.

Meanwhile, Dave was going through a similar process. He had only so much patience and appetite for the New York social scene his wife had grown up in and loved so much. He was a pragmatic man who recognized and truly appreciated the opportunity his wife's family connections afforded him, but he was also well educated and motivated to succeed. He rose in the ranks of his law firm, taking on increasingly important clients of substance. He found a specialty in the mix of corporate and family law that resonated with the needs of a growing band of wealthy industrialists who were starting to profit mightily from the war-effort needs of Europe and Asia.

The United States was not yet engaged, but the handwriting was on the wall. The savvy industrial set was gearing up production capacity while also setting up their families to prosper and/or persevere under any of multiple outcomes. When looked at sociologically, it was a shrewd but concerning skill set. But Dave looked at it pragmatically and professionally. He had great integrity, but no one would ever accuse him of being a populist.

Just as Millie and Dave were gearing up for a great ski season and a pre-holiday getaway to Smuggler's Notch, the Japanese attack on Pearl Harbor occurred. When Dave had spoken to Millie just after Thanksgiving (she had traveled back to Myers for her annual turkey dinner with her father), he had told her that all plans were tentative since it seemed likely that war would break out in Asia. Although he had initially thought it would happen in the Philippines, based on intelligence gathered from all his powerful and well-connected contacts, he had now grown fairly certain that war with Japan was imminent. His intelligence was almost spot on, but the attack was far bolder than he had imagined. Throughout the first half of December, Dave was pulled in for one emergency meeting after another to help wealthy families and corporations position themselves for the coming apocalypse.

Just as suddenly, Millie's world changed at work as well. The government's priorities had to adjust to a wartime pace and cadence. In the world of the New York State Welfare Department, suddenly any thoughts that men should not be the focus vis-à-vis women were shelved. The focus shifted to preparing the boys for war, dealing with the family issues that involved, and starting the process of deploying women for the workforce and leaving their children in someone else's care.

In some ways, the wartime economy was as big a sociological change as it was an economic change. The nuclear family was being exploded, and the cultural norms of homemaker and childcare were being turned on their heads. This made for fantastically interesting programmatic challenges for Millie. She was now truly in her element. This was why she had gone into the welfare business in the first place, and her Cornell training was invaluable in helping her to guide the changes in her small but growing corner of the state.

Millie proved very capable of organizing things such as community day care centers and transportation systems to ferry women to and from factory work, helping the armed forces (which were greatly overtaxed for the obvious reasons) to set up USO stations, and organizing and establishing school and preschool lunch programs to help newly working mothers. She was given a wider and wider mandate from Dorothy to undertake these programmatic tasks over an expanding geography as far south as Saratoga Springs and as far west as Utica and Watertown. Her little Model A saw lots of mileage added to its odometer (yes, the Model A had a modern odometer and even a tripmeter).

While the 1942 spring ski season was lightly attended by Millie and Dave due to their helping in their very different ways to prepare for war, by the following season, things had returned to some semblance of normalcy so that regular ski trips were back on the calendar. During those years, everyone was paying rapt attention to the war effort, especially the various campaigns first in North Africa and Sicily/Italy and alternatively to the island hopping in Southeast Asia.

But a prolonged and distant war was still a matter only of front-page newspaper reports and newsreels to most people. Their direct involvement consisted mostly of greeting returning soldiers and participating in munitions manufacturing. Everyone seemed to be wearing a uniform of some sort. Everyone seemed to have had friends who were lost, and they all mourned collectively. Yet, on some weekends, life went on. There were moments when the burden of responsibilities could be set aside in favor of fun and companionship.

Millie and Dave were adults who had been children of the roaring twenties and teenagers during the Depression. They somehow understood the importance of being serious in their work, yet still taking advantage of whatever free time they had to allow their spirits to soar to loftier climes—in this case, both literally and figuratively. In some ways, the war years provided the perfect backdrop for an affair like theirs. They were each busy enough not to pine for each other, and yet they were both passionate enough to know the importance of an occasional break. They were each oriented by circumstance to live in the moment, and they were each respectful and considerate enough to protect each other's reputations from the social stigma of adultery.

Life went on in this fashion for Millie and Dave as the war ground onward toward victory. On one January weekend in 1945, they were snowed in at a small Tyrolean lodge in north-central Vermont. They did what young lovers do when snow and pent-up athletic energy abound. By March, Millie knew she was in trouble. She had spent enough time dealing with the issue of teenage pregnancy to know that she was with child. While abortion was illegal, one couldn't work for the Welfare Department without knowing how to handle such things. But Millie's Catholic upbringing overcame thoughts of abortion, and she decided she must carry the baby to term.

Speaking to Dave about it was simply not an option. In fact, she skied out the season with him and never let her condition show physically or emotionally. Millie was a tough gal. She spoke to only two people about her situation. First, she drove home to Lansing and spoke to Betty for moral support. Then she drove to Glens Falls and told Dorothy, who was very understanding and simply asked Millie how she wanted to proceed.

Millie was a very competent young woman and had a plan. She asked Dorothy to transfer her in April to Norwich, New York. That was as far away as her manager's territory extended, and it was both closer to Ithaca and far enough from Vermont so that she would have an excuse to not meet Dave as often. And that's exactly what happened. She moved to Norwich, where she knew no one. Her story was that her husband was off to war. No one ever thought to question this since she was a senior Welfare Department employee by then. She stayed to herself except for the occasional visit from Betty. And she told both family members and Dave that she was busy settling into a new job and territory.

Like the Spartan that she was, she worked until the day of delivery in mid-September. She had arranged for an adoption by a Utica family in which the father was no longer able to have children due to a war injury. She felt certain that it was the best way to handle this and never blinked about following through with all aspects of the adoption. The delivery went smoothly, and she never even saw the baby. She would not have even known the sex of the baby since she had signed all the forms with the blanks still to be filled in, except that the nurse slipped up and said, "He's very healthy and in good hands."

She felt that it was time for a trip to New York City. She planned the trip both as a treat for her trials that year and because she had seen all the *Life* magazine pictures of V-E and V-J Days taken in Times Square, which made her want to somehow celebrate the end of the war in New York City herself. She was also intrigued by an article about the Rockefeller Foundation and all the work they were doing around the world. She planned to go to Rockefeller Plaza while in the city. She would also to see Dave, but she was paying for her visit herself and staying at the Waldorf to boot. Such was the strength and resolve that Millie possessed.

It seems an anachronism today, but Millie always wore white gloves when she went to New York. She checked into the Waldorf and had the bellman take her and her small suitcase up to her room. She then called Dave's office and said simply, "Surprise! I'm in New York. Are you free to get together for a drink?" He was more pleased than surprised to hear from her, and her being in New York suddenly didn't give him any concerns. He had known Millie for a decade—a turbulent and thrilling decade at that. He knew this woman and had total confidence in her. If she was in New York, it was for a good reason and would in no way be anything but good for him. He had actually been a bit worried about not seeing her since March and had truly missed their summer golf outings, as infrequent as they were. They agreed to meet at the Oak Room at the Plaza—Dave wanted nothing but the best for Millie.

Millie was impressed by the wood paneling of the Oak Room and the gay and elegant people all around. But she was even more impressed when Dave was given special treatment by the maître d' and received polite nods from several well-heeled businessmen in the room. She was impressed that he seemed totally comfortable walking in with her and that he was so well known in such an important place.

Dave asked how she had been that summer and held her hand on the table the whole time. He was entirely focused on her. He had always had an ability to make whomever he spoke with feel as if they were the only person in the world. She very calmly, and without any perceptible emotion, explained that she had moved to Norwich as planned, but that the reason was that she needed to finish her pregnancy in a quiet town where she was unknown. She paused, and they looked each other in the eyes. She then said she had had the child and placed it with a wonderful and caring young family, never mentioning that it was a boy (she could not see how knowing that detail would help Dave).

Dave squeezed her hand and looked caringly at her, asking simply, "How are you feeling about all this, Millie?" He never asked if the baby was his (he knew it was). He never asked why she hadn't told him (he knew Millie too well to ask). He only showed concern for her.

She replied in a flat and unemotional manner, "I'm fine. It was the right thing to do, and I feel good about the outcome. Now I just have to figure out where I go from here."

They talked for another hour and nursed a few drinks. Millie usually preferred beer, but on this auspicious occasion, she chose to go with Dewar's Scotch, just as Dave had. Finally, Millie said, "It's getting late, and you need to get home." Dave replied with sympathetic eyes that said he really wanted to stay with her. "Right, but meet me for lunch tomorrow at 30 Rockefeller Plaza. I want to show you something." The next day was Saturday, and she had planned only to sightsee.

At 11:55 on Saturday morning, Millie walked into the hallowed halls of Rockefeller Center. She stood in the three-story lobby and stared up in amazement at the murals depicting the Ayn Rand view of the industrialized world. When Dave came into the lobby, he received a knowing nod from the doorman/guard, came over in his tweed jacket, and kissed Millie on the lips. He immediately saw that she was admiring the frescoes.

"I see you beat me to it," he said, pointing up and around at the murals of modern "Progress." "These were painted by a Catalan artist from Spain named Josep Maria Sert." To his amazement, she said, "I know. Sert also painted a Don Quixote scene at the Waldorf." All he could say was, "You never cease to amaze me." She had seen the mural in the Waldorf just that morning and had inquired about the artist.

Dave took Millie up to a lovely table in the Rainbow Room, where he sat again holding her hand. He said, "I have an idea for you." She was always open to ideas, and no one could garner her rapt attention better than Dave. He then laid out his idea that she move overseas for the adventure of a lifetime. He talked about the trip he and his pal Dick had taken to Chile that summer to ski some of the famous Andean slopes that were still pretty much undiscovered. Millie was not surprised by his story in the least. She admired Dave for his adventurous ways. He was talking about South America as if it were the Southern Tier of New York. He went on to say that there was a possibility of a job for her in Venezuela, doing much of the same sort of welfare work she was doing in upstate New York, only in an exciting new country that could provide all the new experiences he knew she would enjoy. As surprised by this new idea as she was, Millie never flinched. Since Dave knew Millie so well, he knew she would be intrigued. What he didn't know for sure was that she would calmly say to him right on the spot, "That sounds like fun. I would do it in a heartbeat if I thought I knew how to make it happen."

Dave reached into his jacket pocket and took out a piece of paper on which he had written a name, telephone number, and address (not surprisingly, right there in 30 Rockefeller Center). He confessed, "I set it up last night. The job is yours if you want it."

Millie said, "But I don't even speak Spanish." The realities suddenly started to catch up with her.

"They put you through an intensive six- week course here in New York before they send you," he said, leaning back in his chair. He had clearly done his homework.

Millie took a deep breath, looked Dave in the eye, and said, "I'll do it."

He quickly said, "Good. I'd hate to think I mobilized someone to come into work for no reason on a Saturday."

She understood why he wanted to meet her there. Some women might have felt that Dave was being presumptuous and manipulative, but Millie did not. She saw his planning as being proactive and thoughtful, but she was still unclear about how Dave could mobilize such things from his law office.

"Millie, earlier this year, I went to work for one of my clients. I'm now the special advisor to the Rockefeller Foundation—and that's who you would be working for in Venezuela. Do you get it now?" he said.

That was that. Millie had survived Tuckerman's Ravine.

CHAPTER 6

Joining the Foreign Legion
(New York City/Maracaibo, 1945–1946)

Millie with her Jeep in Maracaibo

Millie checked out of the Waldorf on Sunday morning with her head spinning. She had spent Saturday afternoon being oriented to the Rockefeller Foundation at 30 Rockefeller Center. Given how flat-footed she had been caught by the whole idea, it was all pretty much a blur. She was initially surprised that she was being oriented and not interviewed. There was a foregone conclusion at the foundation that she was moving forward, rather than considering or being considered for the position. Once again, she was less concerned about such a presumption than surprised at the pace. She began to realize just how much power Dave had at the foundation. He had organized this course of action on Friday night, and by Sunday morning, Millie had filled out all the paperwork to join the organization as a field officer assigned to the Venezuela Office, with arrival in Venezuela scheduled for early January, 1946, only four months hence.

From what her indoctrination officer had told her about the foundation's activities in Venezuela, its interest in the country was largely based on the country's significant oil-production capability, which was making the Maracaibo Basin one of the most productive oil fields in the world. The foundation's interest owed less to any direct linkage with John D. Rockefeller's Standard Oil interests in Venezuela (which had been extensive since 1928) than to the "two-cushion shot" of the Venezuelan Hydrocarbons Law of 1943. This started the inexorable march of governmental ownership and control of oil resources in the country and the foundation's ability to put a good face on the company's involvement in improving the lives of the Venezuelan population.

The Rockefeller Foundation did indeed do plenty of good and important work in development, health, and medical research, and the arts, and few seemed to think it odd that its choice of places to deploy such good works seemed directly related to meeting the programmatic needs of the company that was its biggest benefactor. Millie was as pragmatic as anyone; to her, helping people didn't need to be plumbed for its core values. It just needed to meet a standard of aid and need fulfillment. What she knew of the conditions of the rural poor in Venezuela was enough to convince her that the need was acute and the work done by the foundation was of a caliber that she could proudly embrace—with no worry about its underlying motives.

Such strategic considerations notwithstanding, even more surprising to Millie was the size of the salary she would be making at the foundation. When she graduated in 1937, the average American worker earned less than $150 per month, and the average male college graduate earned $250 per month as an entry-level professional. Due to the "gender discount," when Millie started with the New York Welfare Department, she earned $200 per month, which was more than enough to cover all costs for a farm girl living in rural upstate New York. After nine years and the onset of a labor shortage due to World War II, she was earning $300 per month—a figure that was still $100 below her male peers, but still plenty for her needs. Now, in a casual manner, her orientation officer informed her that her salary would be $9,000 per year plus $1,000 for a deferred retirement savings account, a generous expense account, and a living stipend for food and shelter in Venezuela. She couldn't even compute all this, but it certainly beat the hell out of inching up from $300 per month in the New York Welfare Department, with its 1.5 cents per mile reimbursement for her Model A.

In addition, when she checked out of the Waldorf, she was pleasantly surprised to learn that the foundation officer had called and asked that the hotel bill be charged to their account, referring to her stay as a "recruiting visit." Millie had not come to New York for personal gain, but to do the right thing by Dave. Dave, in turn, proved worthy of her love for him by silently doing the right thing by her on many levels. Mostly, he knew that what Millie valued more than anything was to live a life of adventure, passion, and meaning, and he had set the scenario for her next chapter.

After arriving home in Norwich, a place that now seemed less like home than a way station whose purpose had ended, she started to prepare to leave for good. She would need to drive to Glens Falls to talk to Dorothy tomorrow and then drive to Ithaca to see her father, Aggie, and Betty. She was due to start her Spanish classes in ten days, which meant spending six weeks in downtown Manhattan in an NYU dormitory. It struck her as ironic that after four years at Cornell envying classmates who lived in the dorm rooms, she was finally getting into one. She figured she could combine that six weeks with an extended visit home before her departure date. That would save her some rent and allow her to pare her belongings for the great adventure ahead.

While Dorothy was not rattled by Millie's news (she felt lucky to have had her on staff for so long), she was a bit surprised that Millie would be going somewhere so remote and exotic. Venezuela was a place one read about—but not a place to which anyone she knew would move. Millie's family was another matter altogether. They were genuinely concerned for her well-being. In 1945, with all the tragedy and turmoil in the world over the past decade, moving to a remote, unknown area like Venezuela was like moving to the dark side of the moon, where anything could and might happen. Betty was especially concerned because she read it as a self-destructive or self-inflicted punishment for her unwanted pregnancy. Aggie just didn't get it.

Her father, however, was strangely calm about it. He had left home at eleven for a world as unfamiliar to him then as Venezuela was to him now.

He always thought Millie was most like him of his children, so he settled into the news more with interest than fear.

John Uher's comment to Millie surprised her in its insightfulness. He said, "So you get to do your anthropology work after all." She had never realized that he even understood the discipline much less remembered her interest in it.

Millie promised to return home for the holidays, and she caught the train from Ithaca to New York City with one suitcase of clothes and her heart filled with excitement. When she got to NYU, she was surprised to see that what she thought was a single dorm room was actually a lovely little furnished one-bedroom apartment that had been stocked with supplies and groceries by her new friends at the foundation. She was quite taken aback, having never been treated so well.

As it turned out, her class was an immersion program run by Berlitz and NYU. This meant that it was a seven-day per week program of what was called the "direct method," which focused entirely on conversational and professional capability rather than grammar and syntax. Millie spent twelve to fourteen hours per day in the immersion and took eighteen meals each week with the group in her class. With the exception of a half day on Sunday, she was with her classmates the rest of her time, leaving her little time to enjoy her sweet little apartment. But she did learn Spanish. She had heard in school that if you could dream in a foreign language, then you were fluent. For Millie, the impact was even greater. After six weeks of Berlitz immersion, she could dream only in Spanish.

Before Millie took the train back to Ithaca, she had to spend an extra week with the Rockefeller Foundation's program development team. To her, it was the best week of her life —so much so that she had a break from thinking about Dave, to whom she spoke weekly, but chose not to see. Her days were spent with some of the smartest development experts in the world. She was amazed at how deeply they had thought about the issues of how to improve the lives of people they didn't know. When they went over their theory that development emphasis needed to focus on women rather than men, she almost gasped. To say that she felt like she had found her niche would have been an understatement.

Since accepting her new position, she had studied the geography of Venezuela as intensely as she could from maps and atlases. She knew she would be going to Maracaibo and working with the indigenous Wayuu people in the mountains to the west, near the Colombian border. She was given a report on her charges to help her plan for the challenge she would face.

From: RF Venezuela, Maracaibo Office
To: RF Program Development Team
Re: Wayuu tribal plight

There are a very few places in the world where civilization literally comes to a stop. There is remote, and then there is a null vortex like the area where Central America and South America meet. Many people have heard of the Darien Gap, that area that flows from Panama into Colombia, where the Pan-American Highway abruptly ends. This is a place that is so very hostile to human technology that even a simple road cannot be built or maintained. Man can overcome almost anything, but not everything. The amazing thing about this corner of South America, the part that juts up into the warm waters of the Caribbean and is the northernmost appendage of the continent, is that it represents a study in contradictions.

The Darien Gap provides the umbilical cord connecting South America to the most prosperous continent and is a dense rain forest where vast swampland will swallow any interloper without a trace. Just to the north, things very quickly dry out. In La Guajira Desert, the Wayuu people have existed for centuries in a place others have chosen to ignore. When the desert is unyielding, the Wayuu go up into the mountains to the south and into Venezuela. The Wayuu have elevated their indifference to ignoring the national boundaries and governments of both Colombia and Venezuela. They have no particular disdain for either government, but their lives simply have no use for governments. Such is the beauty of living where others do not covet what little you have. But what man cannot overcome, nature can change in a blink of the primordial eye. Mother Nature can take a dry desert peninsula where the Wayuu could herd their goats and cows in relative prosperity and turn it into an arid wasteland on which the Wayuu can no longer survive.

Our contacts are Luz Marina and Jose Angel, who are married and live in the village of Uribia. The village of Uribia is as primitive as any African or New Guinea locale, with cactus-thatched huts bound together as rancherias and with little more than rope hammock, called chinchorros, and a fire pit. Luz Marina and Jose Angel make their home with their children here though they are considering a move to the mountains. The Wayuu are a matriarchal people so it is Luz who owns the rancheria where the family lives. Luz Marina's father is a palabrero (the one with the "last word"), so she is the informal leader of the tribe. This makes sense since she is relatively educated and has been the village teacher for years. She is one of the few Wayuu who can bridge the worlds by speaking both Wayuunaiki and Spanish.

Her children and grandchildren were raised to a strict standard. They were not allowed to play "roadblock" on the roads to Riohacha and Maracaibo like the other children, who playfully take candy "tolls" from adventurous travelers. Those others are the children who cut school and eventually find their way to the bar/pool hall and form the deadweight of modern Wayuu society.

The Wayuu say that when mankind misbehaves, the god of rain punishes La Guajira. The drought is decimating the assets and livelihood of the Wayuu. Jose Angel can remember as recently as eight or nine years ago there was water, crops, goats, and cows to provide for everyone. Families were relatively wealthy as wealth is measured in goats and cows. Today, there are no crops, and the goats and cows are dwindling rapidly. The Wayuu are now having to buy more and more of their basic needs, and their economy is just not geared up for monetary interaction of this kind. The needs vastly outweigh the means. The drought has had many other effects from children dying of malnutrition to a depressed and demoralized male population who only generally receive a first-grade education. Herding was to be their way of life. Many men just don't know anything else; they only speak Wayuunaiki and are very limited in other skills.

But Luz Marina needs to find a solution that does not just provide a quick fix to the tribe's goat and cow herd size. They need a more permanent home with less severe weather. The Wayuu are a small but proud tribe. Luz Marina has seen the city of Caracas, and that has convinced her that hers is an imported problem that does not end with the Wayuu (she believes modern city life is changing the weather). So the Wayuu must find an answer that does more. Some might say the Wayuu are in search of sustainability. Luz just says she knows they must find many answers.

As with many indigenous tribes, the Wayuu are polytheistic. Most gods or spirits come from nature. The dream world is an important part of their spirituality, and there is a thin line between reality and dreams for the Wayuu. This means that their gatherings, celebrations, and holy days possess a degree of pageantry that is quite unique and colorful. Luz Marina had seen the reactions of the few tourists who wandered onto the peninsula. They are both shocked by the impact of climate change on an entire culture so rich in tradition and then equally impressed by the extreme pageantry of the Wayuu.

Luz Marina's idea is to commercialize the tribal culture of the Wayuu to create a means to replenish the tribal coffers and perhaps allow the tribe to eventually migrate south where the rainfall is still livable. The pageantry of the Wayuu celebrates nature anyway, so it will also carry the larger message. It is a simple plan, but for a largely isolated tribal culture like the Wayuu, it is a monumental adjustment.

Luz Marina and Jose Angel must explain the plan to the tribe members one by one. Group meetings are a product of more advanced governance systems. But the message needs to be embraced, and the villagers must begin to come forward with their best ideas. These ideas so far only take the form of vibrant costumes, exotic dance, and unearthly tribal music.

Luz Marina is not a sophisticated marketer, but necessity is a marvelous motivator. She has traveled to the surrounding towns of Riohacha, Manaure, Maracaibo, and even to Caracas to spread the word that the Wayuu are about to have the celebration of the century and that everyone should want to come and see tribal rituals never before seen by outsiders. It is a desperate plan for a desperate people that are so proud that they desperately work at not looking desperate.

If her plan succeeds, Luz Marina will have saved her tribe. She will have brought attention to a very real and tragic impact of climate change. She may inadvertently strike a blow for sustainability. The cost will be putting her culture and traditions on display and risking a tourism invasion and possibly mockery. It is a risk Luz Marina is prepared to take.

RFV needs to engage Luz Marina to assist her efforts.

In early January, as planned, Millie said her good-byes to her family in Ithaca and boarded the train to New York City with two large suitcases. She had given her Model A back to Aggie, who by now had married Art and was working at their new Red & White grocery on Aurora Street. Aggie had given up driving since she had Art now, so Millie assumed she would just sell the old, but reliable car. Millie went off with the thought that she was more or less leaving Ithaca for good. Such was the nature of development work. This was not a short-term stint; it was a life path she was choosing, and it particularly felt that way as she left Ithaca.

Millie's flight to Caracas was a daylong affair that started at LaGuardia Airport and bounced to Miami, Havana, San Juan, Caracas, and finally Maracaibo. The flights were mostly on Pan Am in DC-3s and Constellations, but a leg or two were on local carriers like Línea Aeropostal Venezolana (LAV), which used an old Clipper to land in Lake Maracaibo.

Upon arrival, a local Rockefeller Foundation employee named Inez met Millie. She did not need to hold up a sign for Millie when she landed since there were only three passengers on the plane from Caracas. To say that Millie stood out would be an understatement. It was midmorning since Millie had overnighted in Caracas, having arrived very late from San Juan. The small hotel near the airport had a very tropical smell and feel, but given her long flight, she fell asleep quickly and easily. She left too early to really form an impression of the country one way or the other. She did note that there was a certain noisy confusion at both the Caracas airport (located by the ocean rather than on the plateau near the city) and the Maracaibo airport (more like a small terminal next to Lago de Maracaibo). What impressed her most was that she had flown over long stretches of dense jungle that were interrupted in several places by mountainous areas. From the air, it all looked virginal with only the occasional red clay road meandering along the logical topographical route. There were no cities or visible towns. If there were villages, they were well hidden in the undergrowth. They had only been flying at about ten thousand feet, so her view of the countryside was quite stunning. The lake had come onto the horizon, and they had landed in the water near the first city she had seen since Caracas. Actually, there were cities on both sides of the lake at the mouth of the lake on the northern edge. Lago de Maracaibo was actually a big brackish inland sea rather than a freshwater lake, but Millie would only learn that later.

Inez took Millie to a small house in a compound of several homes. Millie noticed the Rockefeller Foundation crest in brass on the post by the entry. There was an attendant sitting at the entry, but he seemed more like a friendly doorman than a guard. This was very much by design since the foundation tried its best to fit in without putting their officers at risk. It was a fine line that Millie would tread for a long time. The house was adobe brick with clay roof tiles. The most notable features of the sunny compound were the lush and colorful plantings with flowers almost everywhere. It was lovely. Millie asked Inez if she could just drop her bags and go with Inez to the office. Inez glanced at her watch and said there was enough time before siesta, so she thought it was possible. She asked if Millie wanted to rest or wash up first, but Millie was already getting back into the car.

At the office, Millie met Joe DiFranco and Leonora Corrado, both expats, but it was hard to identify nationalities right away. She also met several of the local support staff. She quickly figured out that Inez was more or less the office manager and sort of the master sergeant of the place. They were all very welcoming, and after a light lunch, the three professionals sat out in the shaded courtyard of the small office building while the staff went home for a few hours of siesta. Millie could see why the staff members needed the break, what with the midday heat almost steaming them under the palm shades. She soon learned that Joe was from Florida and Leonora was from Spain. They had both been in the office for several years and seemed very enthusiastic about their programs and quite comfortable in the tropics. They both lived in the compound where she would be living. Joe was happy to have a fellow American, especially because his wife Marjorie (who was a Detroit girl who just hated he tropical heat) would have another American woman friend nearby. Leonora, as a single woman, was happy to have another single woman. They both spoke

English to her out of courtesy, but when Joe headed off to the men's room, Leonora tested Millie's Spanish. Berlitz had served her well enough, and Leonora was satisfied.

When Millie got back to the compound, it was dinnertime. While Leonora headed off someplace on a date, Joe invited Millie to wash up and come over for dinner since Marjorie was dying to meet her. Millie was surprised to find all her clothes neatly put away for her and her toiletries on the counter by the bathroom sink. She was even more surprised to learn that she had her own local maid who had a small room just beyond the kitchen. She was a girl of seventeen who was shy and self-conscious due to a slight harelip that caused her to look down at the floor most of the time. She introduced herself as Paola.

When Millie arrived at Joe and Marjorie's, she thought she was stepping into a Miami Beach hotel. The fans were blowing across bowls of ice cubes. The air was scented with sweet flowers, and a Tommy Dorsey record was playing that big band sound in the background. Marjorie swept in from the kitchen with a plate of canapés, looking like something out of an MGM movie. She wore a light blue full skirt with layers of chiffon petticoats that had a white belt and a frilly white apron designed more for effect than efficiency. Marjorie gushed all over Millie, asking her if her shoes were the latest style from New York. Millie was at a loss and couldn't even recall where she had gotten them, which was puzzling to Marjorie. It was a pleasant first evening, and Millie could see that she and Joe would become great friends and colleagues. Marjorie sure knew how to entertain, but the tropics were clearly a constant struggle for her.

Millie settled into life in Maracaibo quite easily. The lifestyle was relaxed and easy (she was getting used to sleeping under a mosquito net), and the work seemed interesting enough. But she hankered to go out into the field to get up close to the real work. Disregarding warnings from Leonora, Joe, and especially Inez, Millie jumped into a foundation Jeep and took off for the mountains. The country girl was finally back in the country.

Millie knew from studying the maps where the Wayuu were living in the mountains. There simply weren't enough roads to get too confused. The trick was to not get caught in the mountains during the daily afternoon rain shower. These showers were quick, but quite forceful, coming and going with great punctuality. Inez said they were just to clean the streets, but on the mountain roads, their impact was much greater, making the red clay roads slippery and treacherous.

Millie developed a pattern of starting her days in the field and ending them in the office. Within a month, she realized that she was the only person in the office, and perhaps in the town, who knew one Wayuu from the next. Most importantly, however, she and Luz Marina had become good friends.

CHAPTER 7

The Maracaibo Mambo
(Maracaibo to Caracas, 1946–1948)

Millie, Andre, and a miscellaneous senorita

Millie had flown into Venezuela in early January 1946, and after a few weeks in Maracaibo, she had settled into a routine, allowing herself to start thinking and feeling again. Almost immediately, she started thinking about Dave and what had transpired in her life in the past six months. It had been one hell of a ride, starting with having a baby all by herself in Norwich Hospital, her trip to New York City, and then the ensuing Rockefeller Foundation whirlwind that ended with her landing in Maracaibo alone. Millie was a social animal. With Joe and Marjorie next door and Leonora in the same compound, she was not technically alone, but she was a bit lonely and not yet inclined to seek out male companionship. Naturally, her thoughts turned to Dave. She was hesitant to be too much "in his inbox," but she did, in a moment of weakness, send him a letter at his office.

She enclosed a picture of herself from their last ski trip to Vermont and inscribed the back: "I wish we were skiing, perhaps in California or Chile. Anywhere but Venezuela. Then maybe all our dreams would come true. Let me know when your Dream comes true. —Always, Millie, February 7, 1946

Nothing Millie did was casual. It is clear that she was dreaming the dreams that she and Dave had discussed—dreams about skiing in places other than Vermont, wherever skiing as a sport existed. This included exotic places such as California and Chile, where Dave had been to ski the prior summer in the Andes Mountains. Suddenly all of this seemed much closer to reality for Millie. What were all of Dave's dreams? Had they discussed him leaving his marriage? Millie's closing, "Always," while not exactly emotional, suggested something permanent and enduring. It was an inscription that can be read many ways and—like the trunkful of memories in *The Bridges of Madison County*—it was discovered in Millie's belonging only after she died. No one knows whether she sent it and it was returned to her or if she wrote it but never sent it at all.

Millie lived in the moment, and there was no Dave in Venezuela—and there was so much else to do and see. She threw herself into her work, and the countryside was so different for her and so botanically diverse that every day was a new adventure. One day she would be up in the mountains and the next in the tropical valley or the stark and arid desert of the Guajira. With the exception of the occasional mountain breezes coming off the ocean, the common element of every locale was the heat. Being that close to the equator was something Millie was discovering to be an overwhelming constraint on life. The locals only knew the heat, so they knew to save strenuous work for the early morning or late evening. Millie learned quickly that they were unreceptive to almost anything except a hammock during the midday heat. She did her best not to think about it and coped by washing all her clothes daily (or rather, by having Paola wash them) after only one sweat-soaked wearing.

Her baseline programming was pretty well set by the expert teams in New York such that, with the exception of some local knowledge tweaking, it was hard to improve on in Millie's opinion. Her challenge was to gain the trust of the indigenous community so that they would entertain her suggestions and submit their daily routines to the adjustments necessary to drive productive change. Taking stock of the population was actually the first task since Venezuela had scant resources available for any serious census taking. Given the informality of the border between Venezuela and Colombia, it was fair to say that the indigenous population was a moving target.

She quickly came to focus on the women because the men were unreceptive on several levels and the children were too engaged in the small gadgets of modern life (the jeep, the radio, the ballpoint pen—called a Birome and imported from Argentina). The men were too proud to accept help, too macho to worry about lifestyle needs, and completely unwilling to learn from a woman—even if she was white, came from America, and smelled nice. The indigenous women, on the other hand, were very receptive to anything that would make their very hard lives easier and their children's lives safer. Infant and child mortality was high, and daily life was just plain dangerous in those days in that region. It was not the panthers or wild boars, but the mosquitoes, brackish water, and even simple accidents (which could lead to tetanus) that were the villains.

Millie's approach was a novel one that was decidedly not in the development handbook of the day. She simply talked with the women, asking them what they needed to improve their lives. What became clear was that the needs were very basic and addressable. First, there was access to clean water. This was clearly on the program list, so it was easy for her to resource the task. The men chose where they would live, but the women had to fetch the water. All females from four to eighty had to trek twice daily to the nearest stream and hope the water was clean enough to be healthy. Millie could fix that by helping to better situate their camps (the men were not unwilling to move, they just were never asked), bringing larger buckets to start, and eventually seeing to the construction of simple aqueducts to the village (there was actually a schematic of how to build a simple aqueduct in the RF handbook). In addition, she provided water purification kits to the women, training them to test the water often enough to be sure that upstream pollution was not spoiling the supply.

Almost any problem these people had except for general climate change could be easily fixed, and Millie cut through such problems like a hot knife through butter. It was very rewarding to see how such simple yet meaningful accomplishment could improve so many lives. Even the men started showing her respect, though a formal thank you was simply not in their cultural vocabulary. The children would chase behind her in the village when she drove up and run around her, chirping, "Milli, Milli, Milli" wherever she went.

After about four months, Millie's direct supervisor from Caracas came to Maracaibo to check on things. Alberto routinely sat in on programs that were being run by Joe and Leonora in their classroom at the Maracaibo office. When Millie, who was meeting him in person for the first time, suggested that he come with her into the mountains, he was happy to do so. He had been reading her reports and was impressed with her zeal, but he was dubious that she was making the progress she implied.

After a full day in two Wayuu villages, Alberto spent the ride home grilling Millie about her methods. He had never seen this degree of engagement in his fifteen years in the development field in either Venezuela or Panama. Alberto has been educated at an American school in Caracas and came from a family of European schoolteachers. He was both a dedicated manager and a good soul who cared for people's welfare. He told Millie that he wanted her to come to Caracas in the fall for their annual country meeting (something Joe and Leonora got to attend only every other year). He wanted her to present on her programs and her methods. He was thoughtful enough to also invite Joe and Leonora so that Millie would not become the target of envy.

The meeting in Caracas was eye-opening for both the staff and Millie. She was now celebrated as a fireball, and everyone wanted to be her friend. Her first visit to Caracas after nine months in Maracaibo and the land of the Wayuu was a revelation. She had no preconceived notions about Caracas except for the comments from Joe, Leonora, Inez, and Marjorie. They made it clear that it was a happening town and not dull like Maracaibo. Millie was so engaged with her work and so excited about the newness of the environment overall that it had never occurred to her to think of Maracaibo as dull—until she went to Caracas and took a few vacation days to get a real feel for the capital city.

Caracas was like a cross between Miami and a Western boomtown. The oil finds in the eastern Maracaibo Basin and the western area around El Tigre were thought to be significant so the nascent global oil industry was all over the country. All the geologists and adventuring wildcatters were quick to realize, however, that the place to be was Caracas. It was a lively, fun-loving city, and the nation's prospects of oil wealth made everyone feel giddy and prosperous. Of course, it was all quite a contrast to the severe poverty in most of the rural areas of the country and even in the not-too-distant Caracas suburbs—not to mention the especially challenging situation among indigenous tribes such as the Wayuu.

Visiting Caracas awakened something in Millie that had been dormant for almost a year. She suddenly realized while in Caracas that she had forgotten that her birthday was that week (although her birth certificate and passport said she was born on September 16, her mother had always told her she was actually born on September 14, and that the birth was recorded in the Town of Lansing's ledgers two days later). She was turning thirty years old, which was a milestone. Unlike many other young women who dreaded turning thirty, Millie was totally nonplussed by this threshold, but she did decide that it was time to restart a more complete and more passion-filled life. So she seized on every offer sent her way by the local office team (from both men and women, older and younger) and took a few days in Caracas to celebrate life.

When she returned to Maracaibo a few days later, she knew what she would be driving toward in the immediate future. Her presentation on engaging the Wayuu had gone well, and she could tell that there was something in her naturally outgoing manner and lack of fear that gave her an edge. She decided to write a letter to Alberto and the country director to thank them for the opportunity to share her efforts and methods with the broader team. In it, she subtly offered to be of use in training other field officers in her manner of engagement. As she suspected, they jumped at the chance and asked her to come back to Caracas in a month for a session with several other young field officers. She was happy to do so and get another chance to enjoy Caracas. While back in the capital, she made time to plant several seeds that she might be of more help to the foundation's country efforts if she were more centrally positioned to work with field officers and outreach efforts throughout the country—if she were stationed in Caracas.

Alberto was not fooled by her selfless offer, but he was happy to accommodate her. He had assigned her to Maracaibo because she was a new recruit who had been foisted on him by some higher-up in the New York office. Maracaibo was an office that would do just fine with the likes of Joe and Leonora, whose leisurely pace was perfectly suited to the area. The real jobs were in Caracas. He had a strong inkling that Millie could be a real player in regional development and that her talents merited broader exposure. The fact that she wanted to be in the center of the action was incidental to Alberto's decision. As a macho Latino man, he felt it his duty to the men of Caracas to unleash this vibrant American woman into their presence.

In January 1947, on her one-year anniversary in Venezuela (the foundation was somewhat rigid on time frames for promotion), Millie received her reassignment to the Caracas office. Joe and Marjorie had Millie over for dinner that night (not at all an unusual occurrence). Joe was genuinely happy for her. He was a man who could have done more and inherently wanted to do more, but he would not sacrifice his home life for that purpose. He knew that Marjorie was giving up a lot to let him live his dream in the tropics doing development work and felt he owed her more of his time and attention. He went home almost every day for lunch and doted on her in whatever ways he could. They planned to have children soon, and he knew that free time would be more and more difficult for him to come by. He willingly stayed on the slower path and left the fast lane to worthy colleagues like Millie. Marjorie was initially devastated at the prospect of losing Millie, even though she and Millie were so very different (she could never get Millie interested in decorating or any of her other interests). Then she declared that it was all a good excuse for Joe and her to visit Caracas more often.

Leonora was pleasant to Millie on receiving the news and totally supportive. She did not have a jealous bone in her body, and she was happy doing what she was doing. Millie suspected that Leonora would be happy doing anything anywhere.

In Caracas, she took over a small two-bedroom apartment from a departing staffer. The foundation unexpectedly allowed her to take Paola with her if she wanted to go. Paola was a bit wary of Caracas, but she was more excited than anything. There was nothing to keep her in Maracaibo since most of her family lived far away anyway. While there would be fewer dirty country clothes for her to wash each day, Millie would have many more fancy office clothes for her to tend to. Another attraction for Paola was the abundance of nicely dressed boys in the new neighborhood.

Millie decided early on to get herself properly established on a professional level before taking full advantage of the Caracas nightlife. This had become her modus operandi. In this way, she was sort of half male, taking her sense of self-worth from her success and achievements and half female, liking to be noticed and thought attractive. Her feeling was that she could enjoy the fruits of Caracas once she was on firm ground and well regarded.

Millie very quickly became one of the main leaders in the Caracas office. The foundation was a male-dominated organization, but it had a healthy respect for the role of women in development work. Getting to the valued lieutenant level was possible for a talented female and, indeed, soon achieved by Millie. If she had wanted to be country director, she would have a very steep hill to climb, but as a senior program manager, she was in charge of engagement for all outreach efforts in the country. As she saw it, it was the window through which all success in the field occurred and seemed to her a perfect place to have impact and be noticed every day.

By the end of 1947, Millie felt as if she was hitting her stride in Venezuela. She was known and liked in the office and was starting to become well known in the city since the Rockefeller Foundation was viewed very positively by local politicians and business people alike. More and more people nodded respectfully to her on the street, and she always dressed well to be worthy of those nods. She also was getting noticed by the men in town, and her lack of engagement in that arena only served to make all the hearts grow fonder with the mystery of it all.

She was invited to a big party at the nicest club in town for New Year's Eve 1947. New Year's Eve is always a more festive and important holiday in Latin countries than elsewhere. There is something new, refreshing, and vibrant about the occasion. Caracas was no different, and New Year's Eve was a big deal. Millie went with a large group of friends and coworkers, some of whom had significant others and some of whom were single. It was the way Millie preferred to roll.

Early in the evening, she noticed a very handsome young man talking to some older men across the room. He was using his hands to make a point in a way that showed great confidence. He was holding the attention of the older men who easily had twenty years on him. This and his movie-star Latin good looks caught her attention. She asked a few of her friends who he was, but no one knew. She walked up to him, excused herself for interrupting, and asked if they had met. Though her Spanish was perfect by this time, nevertheless, after a long and sultry drag on his cigarette, he said in heavily accented but good English that yes, he thought they might have met. He immediately nodded to the older men, who were in awe of this demonstration of woman-handling prowess, and turned to take Millie ever so gently by the elbow out to the garden terrace. It was a warm Caracas night, and he looked up at the stars through the palm trees (all of which had been brought up to the plateau in Caracas for effect since they were not indigenous at that altitude). He said he was certain they had met, but just in case she had forgotten, his name was Andre.

Millie's first encounter with Andre left her a bit weak in the knees. In addition to being incredibly handsome, he spoke in a soft, deep voice that seemed somehow more refined than the average Venezuelan accent. It was late in the evening when they met, so they had time for only one dance and one drink to fan the flame. When Millie's friends found her and coaxed her to leave with them, she smiled at Andre and gave him one of her RF calling cards. Andre was very polite and bowed to kiss her hand as she left. He then gave her a knowing wink and nod that were open to interpretation, but his smile told the story.

Millie and Andre partying in Caracas

75

While Caracas was not much by global standards in 1948, it boasted more oil wealth than almost any other city in the Western Hemisphere. Europe and Asia were in tatters and, though most American cities were unscathed, they were recovering from wartime austerity. Rómulo Gallegos had just been elected president in Venezuela's first truly free election in its history, but he would be on the lam before the year was out, trying to find freedom in exile from the country's new dictator, Marcos Pérez Jiménez. Pérez Jiménez was only two years older than Millie and would rule for a decade of development and infrastructure building, all on the back of a booming oil market that supported the country's postwar prosperity. He set the stage for the next phase of Millie's life in the tropics.

CHAPTER 8

Meeting Mr. Wonderful
(Caracas to Maracay, 1948–1951)

Andre headshot

Andre Silvano Marin began life in 1923 in Bassano del Grappa, Italy, a small Tyrolean village just north of Venice. However, he began it as Silvano Andre Prosdocimi, swapping first and middle name in Venezuela years later and formally changing his last name to his mother's maiden name even later, while in the United States. These chameleon-like name changes were emblematic of his persona: "If you … don't like who you are, change it." In Italian, there is an expression, "La Bella Figura," which governs the way Italians think and act. It literally means "the beautiful figure," and it is all about beauty, presentation, and how one comports oneself. It is said to be hardwired into the Italian psyche. The term most definitely best encapsulated who Andre was and what he was all about. His only fatherly advice to his son in his later life would be to "never let anyone but an Italian cut your hair."

Andre's father, Alberto, had supposedly been a senior figure in Mussolini's government, being destined for greatness as the minister of Ethiopian affairs. While there is no hard evidence of this, the fact that he emigrated to Venezuela in the mid-1940s, choosing a quiet little town called El Tigre in which to start a small grocery store, does indeed match the post-World War II "escaping Fascist" pattern. Alberto Prosdocimi was never pursued or prosecuted, so whatever his status and war crimes, they were not severe enough to attract the attention of the Simon Wiesenthal set. Nevertheless, Andre had a Bella Figura story to explain his activities during the war.

Supposedly, Silvano received his military induction notice at seventeen, which was the norm in Italy, as the war was gearing up in 1940. He went through his three-day medical trial and passed the screening as "combat ready." He was sent to his posting assignment on his eighteenth birthday and was scheduled to present himself at a military barracks near Venice. The law at the time said that he had three days to present himself or he would be deemed absent without justification, after which he would be deemed a deserter and sentenced to death.

Silvano had, like everyone in the Venetian area, heard about the University of Padova, and he aspired to go there to learn about architecture and engineering. He had not been a particularly diligent student, so his chances of admission to this prestigious school (founded in 1222) were not strong. Furthermore, as the Fascist machine rolled over northern Italy, the university quickly became somewhat complicit, including curtailing somewhat its championing of free thought and cultural independence. But when the Fascist regime's racism and anti-Semitic laws became clear, the university stood strong against the policies and suffered at the hands of the Mussolini regime accordingly. Andre never had the opportunity to attend or even learn if he had a chance to attend since the war had other plans for him—and the university was too busy to notice.

Andre's story about Silvano's war years was that he was fervently anti-Fascist and pro-American. Of course, this account was provided years later to an American audience as he was vying for American citizenship, but supposedly, these views landed him in military prison in 1941. Given the German occupation of the Tyrol, being anti-Fascist would certainly have been grounds for imprisonment. Being the son of an Italian pro-Mussolini Fascist, however, would have provided a counterweight. In any case, with Italy's declaration of war in June 1940 and the need for troops at the front in both France and North Africa, unwillingness to submit for conscription would certainly have landed a young able-bodied Italian man in prison.

Andre told the tale that he was once taken out with a group of other deserters to the firing squad where they were all given the opportunity for last requests. Only because he asked for a cigarette was he spared while the others were executed. The nature of the man actually makes this story somewhat credible. He was a habitual smoker his whole life, which contributed to both his smooth ways and deep gravelly voice. He certainly was a charmer who could talk his way into and out of almost anything as this story will tell. And one should not forget that as the son of a Mussolini man, he probably was not without some degree of protective influence.

Silvano left Italy with his parents and boarded the boat to Venezuela in 1944, at a time when the handwriting was on the wall for Italy after the fall of Rome to Allied forces in June. Somehow, he had gained his release from prison, perhaps not surprising given the spreading chaos in Italy. He and his brother Louis immediately headed for Trieste to meet their parents for a boat trip out of the danger zone.

In the small, dirt-poor town of El Tigre in Venezuela, Silvano decided to become Andre. As for work, the grocery business was not an option for him since La Bella Figura did not list grocery clerk in its list of acceptable occupations. What became clear to him was that building infrastructure was an important part of Venezuela's future. Despite all the new oil discoveries, roads and bridges were woefully deficient and needed to be built. Had Andre attended Padova, he would have been much in demand for his skills. Although he could not pretend to know how to build a bridge, however, he could—and did—pretend to be a graduate of the University of Padova, claiming that the records of his attendance had been lost in the chaos of the war's end. He was twenty-two years old when he landed, but his smoking and time in prison made him seem older. So Andre insinuated himself into the business of building roads and bridges as a "Padovan," based more on his deal-making skills than on any technical design expertise (for that, he relied on local civil engineers).

When Millie met Andre, he was already a well-established presence in Caracas with his good looks and smooth-talking ways. Serious engineering firms may have questioned his engineering knowledge, but they all stayed close to him since his clout with the government seemed to be growing as he worked his way into the Caracas social set. His story was reminiscent of that of Oskar Schindler, as he took advantage of political autocracy during a time of disarray by being a courtly intermediary. Schindler had done it for personal gain and humanitarian reasons, while Andre seemed to be focused exclusively on the former. Every penny he earned went into nice clothes and his entertainment budget to support La Bella Figura.

While she was at work on January 2, 1948, Millie received from a local flower shop a single orchid from Andre. The note said simply, "Dearest Ludmilla, Meeting you was the highlight of the New Year. Please agree to see me again soon. Regards, Andre." It had the desired effect: Millie was on cloud nine.

For the next five months, Millie rode the whirlwind of romance. Andre was attentive and romantic. He spent lavishly on their entertainment. Nothing but the best for Andre and Millie. And then, within just five months, Andre proposed. Millie had not been thinking marriage before coming to Venezuela—certainly she hadn't considered it in Maracaibo— but something about Caracas and seeing all the young families had made her start to think about a family. Millie was now a sober thirty-two year-old. Andre was only twenty-five, though he seemed a much more mature soul.

For Andre's part, he had never had any problem attracting pretty women. That was somewhat true in Italy and completely the case in Venezuela. His Italian accent and flair worked very well for him with the magnificent Venezuelan beauties. But Andre had become so much more than Silvano now. He had ambitions. His focus was on gaining influence with the Caracas bureaucracy that awarded civil projects. Until he had met Millie, he had never thought much about American women. But he had long had his sights on America. In fact, he had tried hard in Trieste to get his father to consider the United States as a destination for emigration. When he had met Millie, he was struck by her confidence and impressed with her position at the fabled Rockefeller Foundation. He was also taken by her nice clothes and upscale apartment. He was impressed, too, by her educational credentials. He thought she was lovely in an "earthy" way. His access to the loveliest of the Caracas lovelies made him relatively immune to the dark beauties all around him, but he was not immune to the dreams of America that Millie represented.

Millie took one deep breath and said yes to Andre's proposal. She went with him to El Tigre and met his parents and younger brother. While his father was rather quiet (being a man who had made his big play in life only to find that he had backed the wrong horse, lost the race, and had to wear the disgrace of the loss). Andre's mother, Inez, was immediately comfortable with Millie. Inez knew substance when she saw it. Her only question of Millie, asked privately, was if she and Andre wanted children. Millie blushed and said they hadn't discussed it. Inez said that she hoped they would and that Silvano (her given name for him) would support Millie if that were what she wanted. Millie also liked Inez, seeing in her a strong woman who had unquestioned influence over her sons.

In less than two months, Millie and Andre put together a nice little wedding in a small church in Caracas. Andre's family was there, and Millie had Joe, Marjorie, and Leonora stand up for her. She had no wedding dress per se, just a nice cream-colored linen business suit. There was no honeymoon beyond a weekend at a pleasant hilltop resort just above Caracas. In general, their wedding took place in a business-as-usual manner that reflected Millie's serious, career-oriented manner and Andre's almost casual attitude that this event would not change much in his ambitious life.

They lived in Millie's apartment, giving Paola even more clothes to wash and more shirts to starch and iron. Millie was happy, and Andre seemed intent on remaining attentive to Millie … for a while. When he realized how much money Millie made at the foundation, he knew he had won more than one lottery. He was happy and content to increase his leverage in his government business, using Millie and her Rockefeller Foundation connection both socially and by exaggerating his involvement with the foundation.

Strangely enough, the biggest deal Andre had in the works was his effort to win the contract for what would become the General Rafael Urdaneta Bridge, which would connect the two sides of Lake Maracaibo at the mouth of the lake. Andre leveraged help in Maracaibo from Joe, who seemed to know everyone in the municipality. When Peres Jimenez initiated his coup and took power in 1948, Andre cautiously tried to straddle the two competing sides. His father's Italian experience had made him very gun-shy about aligning himself too closely with any one side. In theory, he should have favored Pérez Jimenez, not because of his autocratic ways, but simply because he was all about expanded infrastructure, which would mean more business opportunity for Andre. Nevertheless, by behaving in this way, Andre was able to garner fees from three different companies jockeying for position with the new government.

Meanwhile, Millie stayed on her rocket course at the foundation. Her programs for engagement became famous throughout Latin America. She was regularly flown to other offices in Peru, Colombia, and Brazil for training sessions. By 1950, her annual salary had increased to $12,000. Wanting to make the most of her improved economic circumstances, Millie asked Andre if he would be willing to move to the upscale suburb of Maracay. Anything that felt like moving up the socioeconomic ladder was fine by Andre, so the couple bought a lovely little house with a back terrace that bordered on a tropical "jungle" with monkeys regularly swinging past. Millie loved the Spanish-style house, viewing it as a start to her family plans.

As 1950 got underway and Millie and Andre settled into married life, she got that old familiar feeling. She was again pregnant. This time, however, a sense of calm overtook her since she had secretly been wanting to start a family. It never occurred to her that it would affect her work— and it didn't. Once again, she planned to work practically to the time of her delivery date. This had been a little unusual in Norwich, New York, and it was extremely unusual in Caracas. All of her coworkers advised Millie against it for a first child, but she ignored their advice.

Millie had saved up her leave time ever since she had arrived. She was allowed a trip home every eighteen months, but had yet to take one. Her niece Patty had come to visit her in 1949, and it had been fun to see family. She secretly suspected that Patty was on a family reconnaissance mission for her father and sister, but her niece certainly enjoyed herself as Andre made extra sure that she had plenty of escorts awash in cologne and good Latin manners. The visit served to remind Millie that she wanted her first child to be born in Ithaca. So she put in for two months of home leave from mid-December, 1950, to mid-February, 1951. So much for working up to the delivery date. Andre was very excited about finally seeing the United States and, of course, the birth of his first child.

When Millie and Andre flew into LaGuardia Airport, Andre pressed his face against the window glass, in awe of New York. They had planned to spend two days in the city. After five days, however, Millie insisted they proceed to Ithaca, which they did via the familiar Lehigh Valley Railroad. Millie paraded Andre around Ithaca and Lansing. She was smart enough to stay at the Clinton House rather than subject Andre to too much of her father and Myers or Aggie's deep and likely disapproving glare. Surprisingly, Andre liked the Ithaca countryside. He especially loved the winter snow, which reminded him of his Tyrolean youth.

After the holidays, while Millie nested patiently awaiting delivery of her child, Andre chose to go back down to New York City to check on possible financing for one of his projects. While it is questionable that seeking financing was his top priority for the visit, he did, indeed, set up some cold-call meetings. One of them was at J. P. Morgan, far and away the most "white shoe" of the investment banks. Andre went in and pitched a $10,000 project loan, which, in his portfolio, was a big transaction. At JPM, however, this was a minuscule deal that, as they explained, would not hit their minimums. Amazingly, however, Andre so impressed the JPM bankers that he left with a quasi-commitment for the loan. Such was the smoothness of Andre's world-class sales pitch and congenial manner. Amazing.

Andre headed back to Ithaca at the end of January, having used virtually all of the discretionary cash Millie had given to him. He arrived in Ithaca to learn that Millie had given birth to a baby girl that morning. He went to the hospital like a dutiful husband and father. In 1951, he was not even considered late since husbands were not in the birthing room as they are today. Millie, not liking hospitals very much, had decided to go home with baby Katherine Inez Prosdocimi (a real mouthful in honor of Andre's mother and for the county clerk who filed the birth certificate).

Andre came to pick her up. Before the attendants arrived at her room with the wheelchair, Andre asked Millie for five dollars since he was "a little short." She gave him a five-dollar bill from her purse. The cab fare to the Clinton House was only $2.10, but—true to form—Andre gave the driver the five-dollar bill and told him to keep the change. In *My Blue Heaven*, Steve Martin plays a mobster in a witness protection program. He said, "It's not tipping I believe in—it's overtipping." Millie raised an eyebrow at Andre's "generosity," but she returned her focus to baby Katherine.

CHAPTER 9

Maria von Trapp
(Maracay, 1951–1957)

Governess Maria in Maracay

Once Millie returned to Maracay, she quickly realized that, as much as she liked Paola, her specialties were limited to cooking, cleaning, and washing. Childcare was well outside her skill set. So Millie networked her way into the governess market and found Maria. Despite her Hispanic-sounding name, Maria was German. She had been in country for several years and had the distinct advantage of speaking English, Spanish, and German, all quite well, but all with a strong Germanic accent. Millie liked her immediately because she had a no-nonsense way about her and seemed to understand the lax ways of Venezuela and to be nonplussed by it all. Upon meeting the dark-haired, dark-eyed Katherine, Maria had the temerity to say quite boldly, "This little girl is clearly Daddy's girl." She went on to say, "Maybe the next one will look more like Mama." Millie appreciated the directness. When, during the initial interview, Millie realized that she and Maria shared the same birthday, she felt that she had found her alter ego.

It was a good thing that Millie found Maria. That only became truer on many levels over time. Andre was pretty much useless around the house and certainly around children. He was out and about all the time, using the bungalow in Maracay as a closet and occasional diner. None of that really bothered Millie. She had never been the typically frail female who was lost without her man. Millie paid her (or more accurately their) way with little or no help from Andre. Whatever Andre made from his deal making went into clothes, travel, and entertainment, as it always had. So Millie planned her days, weeks, and life around herself, Maria, and baby Katherine. Maria proved to be a good companion.

Millie's one concession to the macho world had been to take Andre's last name without hesitation. She was not particularly fond of the Uher name, but it took a strong woman to take on an even more Slavic-sounding name from the Tyrol like Prosdocimi. Such things never occupied Millie's thoughts in the least. She could do it, live with it, and even joke about it.

Millie was in good standing with the foundation, but she had risen as high as she could in its Venezuela office. She would never be the country manager in such a male-dominated culture. She diverted her attention away from climbing the foundation's ladder of success, focusing more on getting her family where she wanted it while continuing to guide the foundation staff across the continent to greater effectiveness in their methods of client engagement. Millie liked the work as much as any she had ever done, but she sensed that she was nearing the point of diminishing returns.

Meanwhile, when Andre was in town and at home, he was as attentive to her as ever. She never bored him. She was always surprising him, as one day at breakfast on the terrace, when he watched as a red howler monkey came out of the trees and sat right down and calmly dug into a plate of scrambled eggs she had set on the far side of the table. As he learned, she had gradually trained the monkey to come and calmly enjoy breakfast with them. This was not something he expected from his wife or any woman. She was always surprising him.

So Millie became pregnant again sooner than she thought she would. When Maria learned of this, she just nodded approvingly. She was a keen but quiet observer of the household comings and goings, admiring Millie for her independent, uncomplaining, positive upbeat manner. Millie's expected delivery date would make her next child only eighteen months younger than Katherine. Millie was actually quite pleased with the program. Though some women suffered pregnancy with great difficulty, Millie wore it well and managed it quite well too. Work was fine. Life with Andre was casual and episodic, but fine. She had a routine with Maria and Katherine that worked for her. She knew it all worked because of Maria and made sure the latter was always appreciated and happy. For her part, Maria had found her partner for now and was completely loyal. She quite liked Andre, who was always polite and pleasant with her.

In the summer of 1952, with Ike leading the way in the American election polls, Millie chose to stay in Caracas to give birth to Barbara Silvana Prosdocimi. Her way of showing respect to Andre's family was to always choose a middle name from his side. Barbara's fair-haired looks were as opposite from Katherine as a baby girl could be. Since blonde hair and blue eyes were anything but the norm in Caracas, she caused quite a stir in the maternity ward and in their neighborhood in Maracay.

Now Millie had a regular posse of girls. She, Maria, Katherine, and Barbara went on outings almost every weekend. Occasionally Andre would come along if he wasn't in the midst of some deal that needed his attention. Quite content with his situation, he was proud of his American girls, and it all gave him an unexpected semblance of stability that he found helpful in his networking efforts with the Pérez Jimenez government.

Millie tried to explain to Andre why Pérez Jimenez was not good for the people of Venezuela. She explained how dictatorships were inherently anti-American, but this was all very confusing to Andre, who had grown up in a pro-Mussolini household and only known Italy and Venezuela, two countries that seemed prone to autocratic rule. He had learned to work within such a system and make it work for him, and it was difficult for him to understand that it was all wrong as Millie implied.

Once again, it only took several months for Millie to find herself back at her obstetrician's office. Another baby was on the way. Millie had not thought through any particular family plan, but she suspected that three would be enough for her. Secretly she hoped for a boy this time. She loved her girls, but her male side wanted some equal billing. In fact, from the start of this pregnancy, she was certain it would be a boy this time. If she had worked anywhere but the enlightened Rockefeller Foundation (even in the United States), there would be innuendo that she should perhaps leave her position for full-time motherhood. Of course, few—if any—knew Millie well enough to know that she would never be a candidate for total domesticity. It was strange really to be working with programs every day about how to help women manage their households and families better, yet she was all about outsourcing her own domestic duties rather than taking them on herself.

After five years of marriage, Millie had given up thinking Andre would become a doting family man. At this point, he was actually away more often than not. This didn't affect Millie's daily life too much, but she was determined to get away by herself to have the baby. Given that her due date was in January or early February, she had no intention of going to Ithaca again. She still had her home leave, however, so she planned to go to Florida and use the ticket the foundation provided for Andre for Maria instead. Her standard explanation for the trip was that since she was sure it would be a boy and she wanted him to have the opportunity to become president of the United States. Her Venezuelan friends pointed out, however, that such a plan would leave the boy unable to be president of Venezuela.

Andre understood Millie's plan and had no issue with giving his seat to Maria. He thought of Florida as just a slightly more refined tropical place like Venezuela. He also had great appreciation for Millie's way of not making waves about his lifestyle and choices. He drove them all to the airport dutifully and reminded Millie to call when she had delivered. It was simply what worked for the Prosdocimis of Maracay.

When Millie called her sister Aggie to say she was expecting a third child and would be in Fort Lauderdale in January, Aggie and Art made plans to drive to Florida, a trip they had wanted to take at some time anyway. The chance to see Millie, Katherine, and the as-yet-unmet Barbara was more than enough incentive. Millie had a wonderful and relaxing month at the beach, and then—with her typical ease—she gave birth on January 30, leaving just enough recovery time to be ready for Katherine's third birthday party on February 1. It was an extra-special celebration with the new blond baby boy, Richard Albert Prosdocimi, in tow and riding Maria's hip in between feedings. With his American birth certificate, little Richard departed for Caracas, fully armed to return to the United States to take on the presidency whenever he might be called to the task.

Richard in traditional liqui-liqui suit

Now Millie's clan consisted of one Andre look-alike and two Millie look-alikes. The weekend outings continued with a few added wrinkles since boys were treated differently from girls in Venezuelan society. It was not so much about sports or manly pursuits, which would have been easy enough for Millie and Maria, both being athletes. There were certain things one needed for a young man. For instance, he needed a liqui-liqui suit to wear for special occasions—a white linen "colonial getup" very specific to Venezuela. Other than that, the normal retinue of tricycles, wagons, and beach buckets were all that was needed to get moving through the early years of childhood.

By the time Richard was three years old, the Pérez Jimenez government was showing hairline cracks, with the result that pressure was building against all those who fed off the ecosystem. That definitely included Andre. Meanwhile, the Rockefeller Foundation had had the pleasure of Millie's employ for almost twelve years, making her eligible for a sort of retirement that they offered to field officers. This allowed her to draw as a lump sum the pension funds that had been set aside for her. Together with what she had been able to save from her salary and the value of her house in Maracay, Millie now had a nest egg that could enable her to reestablish the family somewhere. The only thing she couldn't sell was her membership in the proposed golf club of Maracay, which took many, many more years to become a reality.

In the changing political environment, Andre had started to spend more time at home as his other activities grew more and more difficult. Restless, he had begun to talk about trying his hand at the movies—since he was always being told he had movie-star looks. Now the couple began to speak of a possible move to Los Angeles. Millie was more than open to such a move. Her only condition was that Maria had to come with them—and that was it. She was confident that she could work out the rest.

In early 1957, Millie (forty-one), Andre (thirty-four), Maria (forty-one), Katherine (six), Barbara (five), and Richard (three) boarded a liner for New Orleans followed by a TWA flight to Los Angeles. While Andre entered the United States under his Venezuelan passport, Millie had already filed for American citizenship under the War Brides Act of 1945. That formality would occur once they were in California for six months.

Once in California, the family moved into a small rental house in Santa Monica. While Andre went off to find his path to the movie industry and Maria familiarized herself with the surroundings and took care of the children, Millie searched quite pointedly for a business to buy with her savings.

CHAPTER 10

The Art of Deception
(Santa Monica, 1957–1958)

Millie at her Pacific Palisades Gallery

Having spent more than twenty years doing social work for the New York State Welfare Department and the Rockefeller Foundation, and having a family and pocketful of money, Millie decided to zero-base her career thinking. More traditional women of the era might have looked to buy a nice little suburban house within which to raise her brood of three kids. But as was very clear by now, Millie was anything but traditional. So much about her life was atypical for an American woman in the 1950s:

- She was married to an Italian/Venezuelan deal-making movie-aspiring Lothario.
- She had earned more as a development professional than most professional men of her age.
- She had lived and traveled extensively overseas.
- She had supported herself and her family with virtually no marital support.
- She had an Ivy League college degree.
- She had a German/Venezuelan governess in tow to care for her three children.
- She skied and golfed as well as any adventurous man (and still owned a share in a Venezuelan golf club).
- She had lived so robustly that she had had to "join the Foreign Legion" to escape upstate New York mores.
- She had far-ranging and global interests that were not limited to development work.
- She had a deep-seated belief in the imperative of helping underprivileged people, wherever they live.

At this juncture of her life, however, Millie sensed it was time for a pause, or at least a change. She had never been to California, which—strangely enough—reminded her of Venezuela. In fact, the small, rented Spanish-style house in Santa Monica reminded her especially of Maracay. So she settled in easily. Millie was, in fact, just doing what she had always done, adapting to her surroundings with no concern about creature comforts, focused on the next form of achievement.

As a workingwoman who had come to rely on Maria for childcare, since Andre was banging around in Hollywood, doing whatever it was he did, she went off to explore. Just north of Santa Monica, on the bluffs that look up the coastline to Malibu, is Pacific Palisades. It was a more Bohemian community in those years since the real glitterati were in Beverly Hills and Bel Air, where Andre was skulking around, and the more staid inland community of Brentwood was next door. It was in that small village enclave that a small art gallery called simply Palisades Gallery caught her eye.

The art in the gallery was post-Impressionistic with a Spanish overtone, in keeping with the feel of the neighborhood. Millie started talking to Patricia, the woman who owned the gallery. Patricia was older and missed her family from Philadelphia. She and her husband had moved to California for an early retirement, and her husband had simply disappeared one day—never to be seen again. She had gone from suspecting foul play to recognizing that the pattern pointed more toward a quiet and cowardly escape from a marriage that, like so many that had occurred in wartime, never really jelled in the postwar years.

Millie found Patricia a friendly but tragic figure. She had a beautiful home in Brentwood and an inventory of beautiful gifts and paintings in her gallery. She wore nothing but beautiful satin dresses and was beautifully coiffed every day. But Patricia seemed devoid of any substance or desire. She literally had nothing in her life: no husband, no children, no reason for being in California, and no purpose in life. As the two became confidantes over the next few weeks, Patricia told Millie that she wanted to go home to Philadelphia, ostensibly to start over, but really to give up on life. She just didn't know how to do it on her own.

Millie took Patricia on as a project. She helped her sell her house and have her things packed for transport. As for the gallery, Millie hadn't even thought of buying it, but when the issue of disposition came up, there was a problem with the landlord not being willing to break the lease. Patricia asked Millie what she should do. Millie decided, rather abruptly and without any discussion with anyone else in the family, that she would take over the lease. Patricia was so grateful that she sold her the name and contents of Palisades Gallery for a fraction of the value of the inventory. Suddenly, Millie became an art gallery owner.

When Millie told Maria about the gallery, she was very excited. Maria loved art. Andre, on the other hand, simply raised an eyebrow in wonder and shrugged. Andre was indifferent toward art, and certainly toward shopkeeping, but he withheld his thoughts to see what might come of this latest dalliance of Millie's.

On the day of the deal closing, Patricia took Millie to lunch at Chasen's in Beverly Hills—the elegant lunch spot of the social mavens of Brentwood. Patricia expressed great appreciation for all of Millie's help and left her with one piece of advice: "Dear, you need to understand that people who come into the gallery are most often looking for glamour. It's a random and impulsive purchase that they are making, literally with the sun off the ocean in their eyes. You need to add to that glamour not detract from it." She glanced ever so discreetly at Millie's simple, but decidedly not glamorous frock. Millie was impressed with the thought and insight of the comment. She began to wonder whether she had helped Patricia as much as Patricia had helped her in this transaction. She went to Saks Fifth Avenue in Beverly Hills before heading back to Santa Monica and bought two satin dresses that would have made Patricia proud.

While Millie was planning her attack on the art world of Los Angeles, Andre was busy enjoying the high life of Hollywood. He started by having eight-by-ten glossy headshots done by George Hurrell. Andre had seen an article about Hurrell's portrait of Douglas Fairbanks Jr. and had always fancied himself a Fairbanks look-alike. He used all the networking tricks that had allowed him to insert himself into the Pérez Jimenez government bureaucracy. The problem was that movie-star good looks and eight-by-ten glossies (even from George Hurrell) were not exactly in short supply in Hollywood. Andre was finding the doors of Hollywood hard to open.

Maria, meanwhile, was having no problems with the children. Katherine had spent a short time in kindergarten and was heading into first grade. Barbara and Richard were doing what preschoolers do, mostly around the house and yard, which were much safer than Maria was used to in Maracay. Millie was promoting sending the two younger children to a nursery school in Pacific Palisades. All three still lapsed into Spanish at times (as did Maria), and Millie wanted to be sure they were learning in English. She joked that she had the only children anywhere who spoke English with a German/Spanish accent.

Millie was beginning to realize that a governess was simply not typical in the suburban lifestyle in the United States. Furthermore, Maria was suddenly blooming socially, dating both a police patrolman and a local insurance salesman. Millie had grown so close to her over the previous six years that she was pleased that she was developing a life outside of being a nanny. Andre was less accepting since he saw no reason whatsoever for getting involved with child raising at this (or any other) stage in his life.

As Millie started going to the gallery every day, she began thinking about how to attract the right kind of clientele. One day, she was rearranging the art in the shop when a very tall, handsome man walked in and started looking around. When Millie asked if she could help, he said he was looking for a gift for his wife's birthday. She showed him a Spanish medallion on a silver chain that was one of several that she had brought with her from Venezuela. While writing the man a receipt for the purchase, she asked him for his name. He seemed surprised and said, "You don't know who I am?" Apparently, the fact that Millie didn't yet dedicate her Saturday evenings to watching *Gunsmoke* on TV made her unable to recognize her customer as James Arness, the star of the hottest show on television. She apologized, explaining that she had just moved from Venezuela and didn't yet own a TV.

Arness, thinking this was hilarious, went on to chat with Millie about Venezuela as he found her travel and work history fascinating. From then on, Arness became a regular, wandering over from his modest Brentwood home several times a week, usually in the afternoon after his filming was done. Sometimes he came alone, and sometimes he came with his wife. He rarely left empty-handed as he said he always had people to buy unusual gifts for. He also shared many personal stories with Millie, such as his amphibious landing on the beaches at Anzio. It seems that his sergeant insisted he be the first out of the landing craft, using his six-foot-seven frame as a depth gauge to determine how deep the water was. He loved telling that self-deprecating story to minimize his role in the war and because he found it an example of unabashed prejudice against men of a certain size. Millie was surprised that Jim (as she called him now) was the same age as Andre since he seemed much younger.

When Millie took the children to their first day at their new nursery school, she recognized one of the men dropping off his offspring. She had to ask the teacher's aide, who was amazed that Millie didn't recognize Jerry Lewis, all of whose children attended the nursery school.

When Millie decided to throw a party to promote her new gallery, she invited her nursery school parent friends, as well as her regulars like Jim. She had no idea that Arness would bring John Wayne (a good friend of his) and a few other friends—or that Jerry would bring Dean Martin and several studio people. Millie almost ran out of wine and canapés, so successful was the evening. Andre only agreed to come begrudgingly, but much to Millie's chagrin, he spent the evening making a nuisance of himself by hanging all over the celebrities. Andre couldn't stop talking about the gathering for days, and he even asked Millie when her next party would be. He was beginning to look much less attractive to Millie because of his all-too-obvious opportunistic motives.

Strangely enough, that was the beginning of the end for both the gallery and Andre. He started spending more and more time away from home. He also met a few men from a large development company who found his smooth talking ways and deep Italian/Venezuelan accent more appealing than the movie executives seemed to. In no time at all, he landed a job heading the project sales area of the company and was trading in his ascots for white shirts and ties. Somewhere on that path, he met a lovely California blonde, and—with one quick trip to Tijuana—dissolved his and Millie's ten-year marriage. Maybe it was actually a fair trade. Andre had what he wanted, and Millie had her three children and retained at least a small part of her nest egg. As for the gallery, the lease was about to expire, and the inventory was down to the point where Millie could take the remaining pieces home as a fond memory of her foray into the world of Los Angeles and its art of deception. The gallery had actually made money, however, which was more than could be said about Andre.

CHAPTER 11

Ithaca Intermission
(Lansing, 1958–1959)

John Uher (DoDo) with grandkids

When Andre left for the comforts of the corporate life in Santa Barbara with his new wife, Shirley, Millie packed up the Oldsmobile and her brood and headed cross-country to Ithaca, taking the two older children out of school a bit early for just cause in her mind. Maria had settled on Curt, the insurance man, by then. She was happy to have found her life, but she was sad to let the three little ones go. Millie and Maria had been a good team for seven years, but they both knew that, as much as they had leaned on each other, it was time to move on to the next stage of life.

Millie's plan was simply to leave the scene of the crime and go home to regroup. She had gone to California because Andre had a destiny that needed to be fulfilled. Millie had made the most of her West Coast life and had chalked it up as an overall meaningful experience with the art gallery and her Hollywood friends. It had also provided a good life transition for Maria. It had even worked fine for the children as a transition to the United States, allowing them an opportunity to drop their strong Spanish accents in a place where such accents were not all that uncommon.

Millie had mixed feelings about returning to Ithaca. It was comforting to be near her father and Aggie, but she was determined to make it no more than transitional. She had no plan, however—and, indeed, no clue what might lie next in her path. With Andre, she had blown through more than twenty thousand in savings over the previous year. Where some people would have been distraught over such a loss, Millie barely gave it a thought. In her view, money was for living and not vice versa. However, the reality of having to provide for three children meant she needed a job.

Millie was welcomed with open arms by her father. He had been alone in his big old house for almost twenty years since Paul had left for college. There were plenty of dusty but perfectly functional bedrooms on the second floor. As an old farmhouse, the bedrooms were all connected by adjoining doors. There was only one upstairs bathroom with a porcelain claw-foot tub with lots of iron rust stains around the drains. The rooms were sunny, which meant there were always plenty of flies buzzing around the windows. The downstairs was not much better; the parlors and dining room looking unused yet worn from years of sitting idle. The kitchen was from the last century with its wood stove. And down the side entrance stairs was the cellar with spooky-looking farm paraphernalia hanging throughout. It was the home of an old farming man. It was home for Millie too, but it all seemed distant and musty.

After Millie got the children settled and had made the rounds to the few relatives she cared to see (Aggie and Art and Patty and Pete), she began to ponder the future in earnest. She was torn by the conflict of both where to live and what to do, viewing it more as a puzzle to be solved than a problem.

Millie also spent some time at Cornell, chatting about possible opportunities with some of her former professors in the Home Economics

School. They were fascinated to hear about her time with the Rockefeller Foundation and her life in Venezuela. Although she found their offer to appoint her as a part-time senior lecturer flattering, Millie had no intention of staying in Ithaca. That, to her, would be defeat.

While the future decision awaited, Katherine was packed off to Lansing Grade School for second grade and Barbara was trundled off to kindergarten. Not yet old enough for school, Richard was allowed to stay with his grandfather (known by then to the family as DoDo), free to play around the farmyard as John puttered around. Millie knew there was a good chance that Richard would be less well supervised by his grandfather than if Maria had been around and that he would end up eating a lot more hot dogs, but she believed in independence and thought it would be a good experience for Richard—and an even better one for DoDo.

DoDo with Richard on the farm in Myers

Richard loved everything about Myers and the farm. He was only four years old, but DoDo was teaching him how to shoot a .22 rifle, promising that it would be his on his twelfth birthday. Although Millie was strongly anti-gun, she knew this was only a short-term exposure. DoDo and Richard had no trouble finding things to do. They ran around in the fields and pretended to move things in the wheelbarrow. They went up to the garage attic to look for some obscure greasy tool. Sometimes, DoDo would take Richard up to the barn hayloft and show him how to swing on the pulley and jump into the hay. And—as he had done so many years ago with

Millie—he would often send Richard down into the cellar to fetch beer for him, knowing that the feral cats were lying in wait and would likely spook the boy.

This freewheeling lifestyle had several notable downsides for Richard, however. First, there was the lesson about the lack of wisdom of touching the newborn kittens of a feral cat: as he sadly discovered, the human smell made her reject the kitten. When Richard came crying to DoDo about it and DoDo went into the cellar to check on the situation, he came back with a small bundle, which he placed in the garbage. He explained to the terrified boy that the tiny kitten would have died anyway without his mother's attention and that it was sometimes kinder to end suffering. Richard did not take this well and stayed out of the cellar from then on, not wanting to be the cause of any more kittens' untimely deaths.

A second particularly memorable incident held potentially more damaging impact for young Richard. Next door to DoDo lived Agnes of roadhouse fame with her adolescent stepson, Eddie. The boy was constantly being yelled at and yelled for since Agnes was a large woman with limited mobility. Eddie was a poor soul who was basically Agnes's slave in the eyes of the neighbors and carried the additional burden of being raised by a seemingly angry father who needed Agnes as a meal ticket. One day as Richard was playing alone up in the hayloft, Eddie came up and started talking to the boy. As is well known, abused children often grow up to be abusers themselves. Eddie had a plan for Richard. Obviously at the adolescent stage of sexual curiosity, he proceeded to teach the four-year-old about pulling his pants down and playing with himself—to the older boy's apparent pleasure.

Richard had the presence of mind to tell his mother about this strange event since he sensed it was not altogether proper. As a result, a major neighborhood gathering occurred to resolve the molestation. The ever-pragmatic Millie, seeing only minimal harm in the incident—and sympathetic to Eddie's family plight—merely said she wanted it to stop right away. Eddie promised and based on the three smacks to the head he got from both Agnes and his father on the way out the door, no one felt that his transgression would go unpunished.

Kids swimming in the Lansing creeks

Millie was now more acutely aware of the need to make a move. With the winter over, she decided to set her sights on a departure to a destination yet to be determined after Katherine's first communion, set for Easter.

Joe DiFranco had sent Millie a Christmas card the previous December, and it had found its way to her in Lansing. In his note, he had told Millie that he and Marjorie had moved from Venezuela to Costa Rica. He had left the Rockefeller Foundation and joined the Institute of Tropical Agricultural Research and Higher Education. He had added that if she ever wanted to return to the region, she should join him in Costa Rica.

Millie did some scavenging in her papers and found Joe's card. A few calls later, she connected with the institute via a Costa Rican operator in San Jose. Since there was only one place in Turrialba that ever got international calls, the operator quickly succeeded in making the connection. Millie's Spanish also helped the process. As soon as Joe was on the phone, it was as though he sensed why she was calling. When she explained that she needed a job, he was not surprised. It seemed that everyone she knew in Venezuela had seen what she never bothered to notice about Andre and his ambitions. To Joe, it had just seemed a matter of time. He was so pleased to hear from Millie that he never even asked whether she would be coming with three others or four. He just said it was a done deal and that she would get the paperwork later in the week, international mail cooperating.

Millie planned that this would be a stopgap job, so the terms of employment were only minimally important to her. It was good solid fieldwork, and she knew how to do that as well as anyone. The tropical valley of Costa Rica was no concern at all to someone who had lived twelve years in the tropics already and had even raised three offspring while working there. She did wish she still had Maria with her, but that need would no doubt be resolved with local help when she arrived.

The institute in Turrialba was located in a tropical valley two hours east of San Jose. The institute was funded by a consortium of public and private Costa Rican foundations with the common interest of making the rural Costa Rican countryside one of the hemisphere's next big agricultural centers. It was already a significant coffee-, banana-, and sugarcane-producing area. The consortium's view was that the local soil and weather, combined with the country's democratic foundation and traditions, made the area fully worthy of protection and development. One of the tasks was to make the local lifestyle accommodating to migrant workers on a more permanent basis. The peasants who worked the fields and picked coffee beans were not so different from the Wayuu—or very far from them geographically.

Plans were made, and the flight to Costa Rica was booked on Pan Am via Havana. Once again, Millie packed up the kids, explaining that they were moving to Costa Rica. Richard, confused and thinking it was Puerto Rico, of which he had seen a picture with beaches and palm trees, found it perfectly sensible. Aggie and the rest of the family, however, shook their heads resignedly, knowing that Millie would be Millie, with or without young ones in tow. DoDo was wistful about losing his daily farmhand, but he had always known that his bird Millie would fly away again. Costa Rica, Cuba, Venezuela—it was all the same mystery to him.

Millie followed a now-familiar pattern, leaving Ithaca for LaGuardia and another flight south. It was all just another great adventure to the children, another in a string of such adventures. Moving and advancing into the unknown had become a family pattern by this point, but their next adventure was novel—even for them.

It was late April 1959, and Millie had the bad luck to book her flight on the same day Fidel Castro, who was just about to celebrate his hundredth day in power after his grand revolution, chose to fly back to Havana from his first trip to the UN in New York. There was neither an aircraft problem nor a landing problem, but once her plane was on the ground in Havana, there was just too much excitement for the inexperienced revolutionary troops to know how to deal with the still-regularly-scheduled flights coming into Havana from the United States. Pan Am was dependent on its Cuban hub for both Central and South American transit, while the Cubans wanted all the hard currency from Pan Am that they could get, the commercial imperative apparently trumping revolutionary zeal. The American government was still hopeful that it could work with Castro's government, but on that day, the soldiers on the tarmac were at a loss trying to ensure the protection of El Jefe.

All of the passengers were herded into a small transit shack at the airport. In that shack was a small souvenir shop that had suffered diminished inventory from the months of commercial disruption. Millie had always collected things for the children so they could appreciate where they had been. The girls collected the ubiquitous local dolls, and Richard collected boats or ships. On this day, the little souvenir store had a boat but no dolls. Millie made the mistake of buying a boat for Richard. Whereas Barbara was content thanks to a coloring book, Katherine—a rather expressive, headstrong young lady—threw a fit. Oblivious to the guerrilla tensions at the airport, she ran pell-mell out of the shack and onto the tarmac. She was followed on the run by a Cuban soldier with a US military war surplus M1 rifle, who was followed by Millie, who was followed by Barbara and Richard, who were followed in turn by a very nervous Pan Am official. Amazingly, no one got hurt, despite considerable yelling and screaming. Upon reentry into the shack, no one was testier than Katherine, who still wanted her goddamn doll.

Eventually, Fidel arrived safely and was escorted back to Havana, and the sequestered passengers were sorted out and boarded various planes to Central America as planned. Millie and her children proceeded on to San Jose along with one seashell boat and one very pissed-off young lady.

CHAPTER 12

Back to the Tropics
(Turrialba, 1959–1961)

Kids in the Turrialba backyard

As the Pan Am *Constellation* made its approach to San Jose's Aeropuerto Internacional el Coco, Richard looked out the window and saw first miles of jungle, then a big mountain with smoke coming out the top, and finally tin roof after tin roof as the plane descended. He wasn't seeing palm trees, beaches, and swimming pools—just lots of tin roofs. He turned to Millie, who generally sat with him while his sisters sat together across the aisle. "Why are all the roofs metal, Mom?" he asked.

Distracted by the details ahead of her, Millie only mumbled something to him, so he moved on. He began to think he might have made a mistake in assuming that Costa Rica was a tropical paradise.

Nothing about this relatively new airport in San Jose felt unfamiliar to Millie. After twelve years of coming and going from the tropics, the disarray of the airport was no surprise. But the kids had been away from the tropics for almost two years, which is a lifetime to a child, and this did not feel like Los Angeles or Ithaca. It felt foreign and so exotic that they felt a need to stay quiet and close to one another. No one met them, and Maria wasn't there to help them while their mom organized the luggage.

Millie got them and their luggage into a taxi that had the strange sweet smell of overripe fruit. The driver kept an array of mangos, bananas, and guavas on the dashboard. There was also a strange reddish fruit that looked like a pear. Millie asked the driver what it was and was told "manzana de agua," which meant "water apple" in English. She had never heard the term in all her time in Venezuela. She and the children were to enjoy this unique fruit for their entire stay in Costa Rica yet never see it outside the country. As the taxi pulled up to the Gran Hotel, the group's focus shifted to the white-gloved doorman.

All staff at the Gran Hotel Costa Rica wore sparkling clean, white gloves. This was an amazing colonial hotel with slowly turning ceiling fans, long cloistered colonnades, and louvered doors and windows that gave the whole interior a feeling of being shaded and cool in an otherwise hot, dusty city. There was no hustle and bustle in the hotel. Everything had a calmness and elegance that almost canceled out the sense of chaos that the airport had cast on the children.

Millie was less impressed since she had seen this sort of contrast in Caracas, but she was glad to see the kids seemingly relieved and less in shock. As the two bellmen helped them to their suite with its basket of fresh fruit, Millie asked about a pool and was told there was a small one in the courtyard. She felt this assignment was going to work out just fine.

After a few hours at the pool, all three children were sufficiently worn down to remember the training they had received from Maria, and they cleaned up and dressed for dinner as only little Latin "pequenos" could. Maria, a Germanic force of nature, had prepared her charges well with respect to dinner comportment. They marched in orderly fashion down to the dining room with Millie, and five-year-old Richard knew to hold out his mother's chair for her at the table. Katherine and Barbara sat like angels with their hands in their laps. Even Millie was impressed. It seemed as though every patron in the dining room was smiling at this American family whose members seemed so comfortable on their first night back in the tropics.

At ten the next morning, the van that would drive the family to Turrialba arrived, looking less than elegant with its side panels reading CATIE—Centro Agronómico Tropical de Investigación y Enseñanza. The phrase was partially obscured by mud from the morning jaunt into town. Getting to Turrialba required an hour-long ride on a busy commercial road to the colonial town of Cartago, followed by a harrowing trip along a mountain-hugging road with banana and sugarcane fields on each side that passed through mountains covered in coffee trees, which finally opened onto a tropical valley.

Though it was all visually interesting to the children, Millie saw a remote town with a few very scruffy shops and almost no paved roads. She had seen it all before, but the impact was heightened by having only so recently left Santa Monica and Ithaca. Not until the van passed through the town and headed a mile east to the institute grounds did she feel some relief.

The Turrialba institute

The campus actually looked quite civilized as they drove through the well-manicured entrance and around the large lily pond. On a small knoll to the right sat a house that the children immediately concluded would be their new home. Millie knew better. The driver explained to her in Spanish that this was the director's house, as she had assumed. He then drove up to the colonial administration building on the far side of the pond and brought the now-even-muddier van to a halt.

In the time it took Millie and the kids to disembark, several people—including Joe DiFranco —had emerged from the building. After warm greetings and introductions were exchanged, Millie and the children were escorted into the building lobby, where a pleasant luncheon had been laid out for the newest member of the institute staff and her family. Millie met the director, a pleasant, older Dutch gentleman of rather regal bearing. The staff she met at lunch seemed to be evenly split between local Ticos (what Costa Ricans called themselves) and foreigners, once again approximately evenly split between Americans and Europeans.

After lunch, Joe walked the family back out to the van where the driver was dutifully waiting. Joe hopped in the front seat next to the driver, directing him to drive to his house. "Marjorie would never forgive me if she wasn't our first stop," Joe sheepishly explained to Millie. She was very pleased to see Marjorie—and even more pleased to see the cool tile and modern refrigerator, complimenting Marjorie on her tidy home. That only caused Marjorie to launch into how hard life was in Turrialba compared even to Maracaibo. Apparently her American refrigerator had practically been declared a national asset when it had arrived in San Jose from the manufacturer in Dayton, Ohio. But she was clearly happy to see Millie and the youngsters, who, she remarked, had grown "so much." When Millie asked about her son and daughter, she explained that her boy was in a military academy in Florida and that her daughter had insisted on going to school in San Jose, where there was a fine girls' boarding school for just such purposes. That left Marjorie in her little tropical valley to take care of Joe and "beat back the tropics." She said that on any given day she felt certain that the tropics were winning the battle and would undoubtedly win the war. Millie smiled and remembered how much she liked Joe and Marjorie.

While Marjorie entertained the children, Joe sat Millie down and explained that she would have to live in a small three-bedroom house just off the grounds while the institute completed several newer homes for staff on the grounds. Millie could expect to be given one of the new homes by the end of the year. The children would all go to the school on the institute grounds, which housed grades one through eight. Younger students went to kindergarten in town, and the older ones attended boarding schools in San Jose or overseas. Marjorie had already found Millie a maid who would live in in a small room off the kitchen that all houses in the area seemed to have. As for the work, in typical fashion, Joe treated it as a secondary matter behind the family necessities, noting that the goals and methods would all be familiar to her. As usual, he explained, there was lots to do and, fortunately, no shortage of resources since the founding members' motivation was mainly commercial and their focus was on improving the region to advance their vast agricultural interests. Although rural land reform was not on the agenda, there was nonetheless plenty of good work to be done. He ended by saying that he and Marjorie were building a good life here—and he was sure she could too. He ignored the two elephants in the room of Andre's absence and the unquestionable fact that this was just a temporary assignment on Millie's march to wherever she ultimately decided to go.

A stark contrast in both look and feel presented itself when one left the institute grounds, even by a mere three hundred yards to the temporary house assigned to Millie. The nicely groomed vegetation was replaced by a combination of planted cane fields that ran right to the roadside and vast stretches of banana trees that looked like untamed jungle. In between had been hacked a bit of spare dirt with a few houses made of cinderblock with the ubiquitous tin roofs. When the family pulled up to the house on the rough gravel road, all the kids could see was the tin roof. There was a manzana de agua tree in the backyard as well, and that alone proved to be a blessing as the whole family came to love the indigenous tropical fruit.

The house proved adequate for their needs, and the family's adaptability allowed them to settle in quickly. The maid appeared to be perhaps sixteen years old (even she was not certain of her age), and she was almost pure Indian. She was quiet but clean and had chosen the name Ana since her real name was an indecipherable indigenous one. She helped the family the best she could, largely staying to herself. One day each week, she walked away through the banana trees with her weekly stipend, presumably to share her good fortunes with her family at home.

While Millie settled into her job, the children, under Katherine's leadership, prepared for one of the great unfair tragedies of life. Given Costa Rica's closeness to the equator, its school calendar ran opposite to that in the Northern Hemisphere. That meant that, while the kids had just finished their school year in Ithaca, the school year was in full swing here. Richard, having not yet begun school, was unaffected. Barbara, for her part, was happy to draw wherever she was told to be. Katherine was characteristically indignant, loudly expressing her distress at the dinner table. Millie listened carefully and—knowing her daughter—observed that this would only help make Kathy smarter than all the other kids. This was just the right response to make to the prideful young girl. She never again mentioned the issue, certain that her superiority would be even further enhanced by more schooling.

The next day, Ana took the children into town to shop for groceries. It was a trail of one little scruffy shop after another until they entered a big square that was filled with market stalls with every kind of organic local food product imaginable. The strongest impression on the children was made by a vendor of sweet rolls. There were stacks on stacks of sticky buns with raisins. When Ana asked for a few to take back, the vendor waved his hand across the stacks and all the raisins flew off, buzzing as he bagged a few of the rolls for Ana. The flies then slowly landed again across the stacks, again becoming raisins. Duly noted.

Millie was concerned to find a church for the children. One visit to the local Catholic church with its chickens and pigs and Latin dirges convinced her to follow the DiFrancos and the other Americans to the small mission set up by a family of Iowa Presbyterians. Thus did Millie and her kids become Presbyterian—largely as a matter of cultural convenience.

Richard was sent off to Turrialba's one and only school, which allowed five-year-olds to spend the day in something resembling kindergarten. The eighteen months spent in the United States had made the children's Spanish rusty, but they quickly regained their fluency. Richard was driven by the same van driver every morning the two miles into town and picked up five hours later before siesta. The time in between was spent largely running around the playground with an occasional indoor storytelling session. Richard had a big problem: he was blond, which made him unique in this tropical valley of jet-black-haired people. To obscure this distinctiveness, he took to wearing a hat similar to a British motoring cap, but he was still odd man out of all activities and generally put upon in a friendly but taunting way.

Being an ingenious lad, Richard hatched a plan to remedy his problems. It made perfect sense to him that if he were to cut off his blond hair, there was a better than even chance that it would grow back darker. One afternoon, he located a pair of scissors and went at the front shock of his hair. That was the part that his mother kept pushing over and upward on his head while referring to how someone called Jack Kennedy wore his hair. Richard made short shrift of his Jack Kennedy lock of hair and looked at his handiwork admiringly in the mirror. Now all he needed to do was wait for the darker growth to come in.

When Millie got home and saw her grinning male child with the butchered hair and the two girls intently playing jacks in the living room to avoid any possible connection with the incident, she sat down and cried. Millie didn't cry over many things. She was strong and brave and rugged. But like everyone, she had her trigger points—and this latest evidence of her inability to control her environment proved an overload point. She rallied quickly, however, writing a note in Spanish for Ana to give to the van driver in the morning. She then put the kids and herself to bed.

The flaw in Millie's plan became evident only after she had left and Ana and the van driver puzzled over the note as only two illiterates could. It had asked that Richard be driven first to the barber for his hair to be trimmed before school. Ana's field decision was correct: certainly Millie wanted the boy taken to the barber. That much was clear without words on paper. As it turned out, however, the barber, too, was illiterate, so he took up the task as he would have for one of his children and simply shaved the boy's head to the scalp.

Richard was too intimidated by the whole regimen that morning to do anything but submit. When he saw the stark results in the barbershop mirror, he could only be thankful that he had his cap, which he promptly pulled down as far as it would go. The driver then dutifully dropped him off at the playground while Millie was sitting through a heavy meeting at the institute about how to empower local women to improve the lives of their families. It took perhaps two minutes on the playground for this tragedy to unfold. A favorite game had been chasing Richard and grabbing his cap to make fun of his blonde hair. Today there was a new surprise in store for the forty or so dark-haired boys running around the playground. When the cap came off it was like an E. F. Hutton ad—everything stopped and went quiet. Then some kid shouted, "Coco Pelado," and soon the whole playground erupted in laughter, with everyone running around Richard screaming, "Coco Pelado, Coco Pelado."

That day, in response to a call to the institute from the local school, Millie went herself to pick up Richard. The surly boy with the cap pulled down unnaturally to his ears jumped into the car and told her to take off. Hearing the children yelling something at the car, she drove off, but she then stopped by the side of the road and asked Richard what they were saying. He took off his hat and explained that they were calling him a bald coconut, adding that he was never going back to that school … ever.

Richard started a bit early at the one-room schoolhouse on the institute grounds. He proudly told the older children that he had "dropped out" of kindergarten. At night, Millie would see him looking in the mirror at his slowly returning head of hair, and he would ask, "Does it look like it's coming in darker?" Though riddled with motherly guilt, Millie consoled herself with the thought that what didn't kill him would indeed make him stronger.

What could actually kill him, however, was any of the poisonous snakes, frogs, and wild cats that inhabited the lush valley of Turrialba. In general, Millie had little fear of her physical surroundings, but without strong support from someone like Maria, she occasionally found herself wondering if the children had sufficient supervision in this challenging jungle setting.

One day her worst fears in this regard were confirmed. The kids' walk home from school was short enough that she believed Kathy could adequately supervise her younger siblings on the short trek. Once home, Kathy had homework, Barbara liked to stay inside drawing or painting, and Richard played out in the road with several other boys. He had just recently learned to ride a bike by being pushed down a small grassy school yard hill. This crude but effective approach was akin to being thrown into the deep end to swim. Bike riding on the gravel road by the house was a favorite pastime. On this day, Millie found Richard riding his bike up and down the road dragging a seven-foot Bushmaster snake behind his bike. It seems a gardener had discovered the extremely venomous snake in the backyard (they are partial to bananas and the spiders that inhabit them) and had killed it. The boys thought it would be great sport to flaunt the kill by tying the carcass to the bike. Little did they know that the snake's venom was so poisonous that had they touched it near its sliced head, they could have been blinded—or worse.

Sometimes the dangers were more self-inflicted. Lassoing banana trees and pulling down great green bunches of bananas seemed a good use of an afternoon and a rope. While suburban American children were getting sick on green apples, Millie's kids were getting sick on green bananas, washed down with a dessert of raw sugarcane. This had the combined impact of turning the children's intestines rock-hard for a week and their teeth a light shade of brown from almost immediate organic decay. The San Jose pediatric dentist built his business model entirely around the effects of sugarcane chewing. Millie's children contributed to keeping him busy with their blossom of cavities from sugarcane and the lack of fluoridation in the local water supply. For years to come, their teeth and digestive tracks would bear the marks of this particular tropical sojourn.

Costa Rica in 1960 was an archaeological gold mine of pre-Colombian artifacts. Located in the narrow pathway between the early Aztecs and Incas, it seemed to have been a popular place for pre-Colombian Indians to bury their dead. Though the country was filled with burial mounds, the government had yet to get thoughtful about the preservation of antiquities. As soon as the locals began to realize that foreigners found value in pottery and pomace sculpture, beyond the obvious interest in any gold artifacts, an active local market sprang up in grave-robbed artifacts. It was a rare day when no one showed up at the door of Millie's home with an old cloth covering a clutter of pieces with earth still clinging to them. The cost was less the issue than finding space to store the pieces. Millie saw no harm, however, in selectively buying interesting pieces and then just piling them in an old box in the back room. It was her nod to her past and somewhat abandoned interest in anthropology.

She used the fruits of this local archaeology to create a teaching moment, motivating Richard to take up a new hobby. This led her occasionally to send him off with a male coworker or subordinate for weekend dig expeditions, which seemed both educational and manly at the same time. The booty from these expeditions was just more loot for the old box out back.

Ultimately, while Millie tried to make the most of her Costa Rican opportunity both for her children and herself, she knew from the first month that despite Joe DiFranco's earnest suggestion that she build a life in Turrialba, she would have to look elsewhere for her destiny. By New Year 1960, Millie had decided to return to school for her PhD. She had read about Margaret Mead and her groundbreaking work in anthropology, and she decided that she needed to make an impact on the world in her own way.

To do this, she would need to find a generous financial aid package and the right program, but she set about her search while continuing to hone her fieldwork skills in the hills around Turrialba. She was now sure that she wanted to be an educationalist and study the dynamics of programmatic aid efforts on indigenous populations. Her twenty-three years of experience in the thick of the field (domestic and foreign) combined with an Ivy League degree made her an interesting candidate for many programs. Her age (forty-four) with three children, however, made her a more challenging degree candidate than most. Nevertheless, the University of Wisconsin seemed to have a perfect fit for her that went well with its strong commitment to diversity. As for the children, they just went along for the ride no matter what their mother wanted. Costa Rica was fine, but the United States with its TV cartoons and plentiful ice cream seemed pretty fine too.

The tropics had tried to woo her into its clutches as it had wooed Joe and Marjorie. Their daughter Mindy got so culturally entangled, in fact, as to marry a Tico and take up permanent residence, much to Marjorie's chagrin. Millie could put up with the snakes, spiders, and flies, and she actually felt the one-room schoolhouse could work well for the children for at least a few years but not for more. The institute work was fine, but it was uninspiring. The tropics would therefore have to release its grip on Millie and her family. The four were soon headed north to the land of ten thousand frozen lakes and solid Midwestern values that they had learned to appreciate in the midst of their Presbyterian friends in Turrialba. Millie may have initially used the tropics as an escape, but now she was seeking to escape from the region's grasp.

CHAPTER 13

Suburban Badgers
(Madison, Wisconsin, 1961–1965)

Richard in front of suburban Spring Harbor home

Madison, Wisconsin, is the capital of the Dairy State and the main campus of the University of Wisconsin Badgers. It sits between two lakes, Lake Mendota and Lake Monona, where ice fishing and ice boat sailing are the favored winter sports. These sports are decidedly nontropical—as is the state of Wisconsin altogether.

Millie and the children arrived in Madison in August 1961. This was the year of Camelot in the United States, and higher education was a clarion call for all to follow. President Kennedy could read 1,200 words per minute, and God help anyone who couldn't keep up. Millie had made one advance trip to Madison to buy a 1956 teal and white Oldsmobile and rent a small two-bedroom house in a picture postcard suburb. The house was the size of the family's first temporary house in Turrialba, but it rented for only a hundred dollars per month and was within walking distance of a good suburban school. There would be no Ana or Maria in Madison, so walking distance to school was important. Millie would be working from what little savings she had and a $3,000-per-year fellowship stipend. After the rent was paid, only $150 per month remained to spend frivolously on utilities, food, and clothing.

The house was exactly the sort of peaked-roof house drawn by any first grader. There was a door in the middle with one window on each side and a small chimney on the roof. Perhaps a thousand square feet with a full unfinished basement and attic, it had a living room, kitchen, bathroom, and two bedrooms. One bedroom was set up with a bunk bed for the girls, and the other had a bunk bed for Millie and Richard (who got the top bunk without argument). There was a wall telephone in the kitchen but no television—at least not yet. There was also a Presbyterian church nearby. The house had a big backyard with a crab apple tree that looked down on a highway into town. Perhaps its greatest asset was a surrounding neighborhood filled with other kids to play with. Notably, it also had paved streets and no jungle, bananas, sugarcane, or coffee plantations and roasters. In other words, it was a palace in a paradise that had everything the family needed.

After only a week of indoctrination, it was time for the children to start back at school. This was a shock to Richard's system since it seemed like he had been going to school forever, or at least since March. Kathy explained it to him in a mildly condescending way—as only a fifth-grade older sister who had been through the Northern/Southern Hemisphere program could. Barbara was enrolled in third grade, and Richard was in second.

On his first day at school, when Richard was asked to put his name on a paper, he wrote it out in his best cursive as taught to him in Turrialba. The teacher told him he needed to print and not use handwriting, which struck him as strange since he had been told the exact opposite in the little one-room schoolhouse. When the teacher asked how many ways there were to make the number six, amidst all the 2 + 4, 1 + 5 and 3 + 3 answers,

Richard said, "Two times three." The teacher was apparently not pleased by this answer. Then came the final straw: spelling. Richard was careful to print this time, but when asked to write a word about his summer, he wrote the word c-o-m-m-u-n-i-t-y, a word he had learned in school several months before. It seems that we tend to underestimate the potential value of a one-room, first-through-eighth-grade schoolhouse where the teacher has more older than younger students. The younger ones just sponge up the bits and pieces.

During recess, his second-grade teacher held an impromptu conference with the principal and handed Richard a note to give to his mother that night. Millie went to school the next day, missing a class of her own to do so, but what else could an aspiring educationalist do under the circumstances? Richard was in the room, trying to follow the conversation between the teachers, the principal, and his mother, but he could only make out that he was somehow doing something wrong that he had learned in Costa Rica and that his sister Barbara was somehow involved. His mother was not mad, but she did question the teachers and occasionally looked back at Richard with a smile.

When they finally finished, his mother said he should go with the teacher (not the one he had been with yesterday) to his new classroom. He would be going into third grade, but not the class that his sister was in. Richard shrugged and asked if his new friends Larry and Dan would be in that class. He was told no, but that he could see them at recess.

That night, Richard quizzed his mother about what it all meant, and she explained that he would be wasting his time in second grade and that the teacher was concerned about his upsetting the rhythm of the class curriculum because he already knew so much. He said that he was a little confused and worried that he might be behind in third grade. Millie was conflicted about the whole thing, but she decided it was for the best, mostly because of the attitude of the second-grade teacher, which seemed rigid, to say the least. With another shrug, Richard went back to lobbying his mother for a TV since everyone else in the neighborhood had one.

At forty-four years old, Millie would probably have felt ancient in any department on campus except for the Adult Education Department. While most doctoral candidates were not as old as her, they were almost all ex-teachers who had worked for at least ten years. This made her less an anachronistic oddity than an interesting experienced colleague. There were even several foreign students, but clearly none had spent time in such exotic parts of the world as Millie had. All of this served to give her status of sorts, and her best friends became some of the professors nearest her own age and the more experienced grad students.

One of the requirements of her fellowship was that she taught undergraduates. Somewhat understandably, given her background, the department assigned her to teach a course titled "How to Study." What was strange to her about that was that, as someone who was twenty-three years from her last class, she felt she probably needed the course more than the students did. Task-oriented Millie developed a course syllabus from scratch, based simply on common sense and her knowledge of the general process of learning. She drew on many of her old high school tricks as well as bits and pieces that she had used to develop training programs at the Rockefeller Foundation.

After receiving rave reviews from her students in her first semester, Millie wondered if she had missed her calling as a teacher. Word of her abilities spread quickly on campus, and enrollment in her course mushroomed. Her department head took notice and asked for a copy of her course materials, which was quite unusual for a first-year grad student. Once again, Millie was making her mark early on.

Meanwhile, the situation on the home front was settling into a groove (as opposed to a rut). Millie had relented and bought a used television with what seemed to be a five-inch screen set in a four-foot wooden cabinet. It was sufficient, however, to enrapture the children, as episode after episode of *I Love Lucy, Gunsmoke,* and *Have Gun Will Travel* rang from the rafters. Even Millie occasionally took a break from her heavy workload to watch her old pal Jim Arness on *Gunsmoke.* Santa Monica and Pacific Palisades felt like two lifetimes ago to her at this point, and it was almost surreal to think that she used to joke around in her gallery with the biggest star on prime-time television.

Instead of art and expensive gifts, her focus was now exclusively on the basic requirements for her doctorate. By this time, she had nearly completed her master's degree requirements and even written her thesis on adult education in development. Now she was moving into finding a dissertation topic and fulfilling some of the more archaic doctoral degree requirements such as statistics and foreign languages. No one in the department was as fluent as she was in Spanish, but the requirements included proficiency in a second foreign language as well. She had no time for an additional class, so she bought a book on French, studied it day and night for three weeks, and then took and (barely) passed the proficiency exam. When Richard asked her about it, she said very pragmatically that it was an outdated rule and that languages would be obsolete someday. This came from probably one of the few women in America brave enough to take a six-week immersion course in Spanish and thrust herself into a country like Venezuela, where English was barely spoken.

The Spring Harbor Elementary School, which all three children attended, was a crab apple-on-a-stick's throw from their house, but between them ran University Avenue, the highway visible from the backyard. To connect the school to the housing development, the city planners had placed an underpass made simply of a corrugated steel tube with a poured concrete floor and a string of galvanized steel industrial light fixtures running its length. All the elementary school children who lived south of University Avenue went through that underpass four times a day (since there was no lunch served at school). A popular boys' sport after school was to throw rocks down the tunnel of the underpass to hear the pinging sounds they made on the corrugated metal. Though Richard found this silly, he was desperate to be accepted by his older classmates. When he finally threw one rock, it hit a lamp fixture, bringing it down in a shower of sparks as the boys scattered to the four winds, laughing as they went.

When the police showed up the next day at school and started pulling random hoodlums out of class for questioning, the only thing anyone could remember about vandalism in the tunnel was Richard throwing a rock and destroying the entire tunnel lighting system. When the letter from the police arrived on Millie's doorstep, she began to think that perhaps the snakes and spiders of Cost Rica were less dangerous than the American suburbs. She was now a doctoral student mother to a juvenile delinquent, as duly referenced by the Spring Harbor Police.

Millie needed to start thinking about the summer when the children would be out of school for three whole months, and she had a dissertation to outline. The girls would be fine at the local community day camp at the park, where they could braid "gimp" (plastic lanyard) to their hearts' content. But Richard needed a camp—and camps cost money, of which Millie was woefully short. Richard solved the problem himself after hearing at school about the YMCA camp that a student could attend simply by selling enough YMCA chocolate mints. Richard sold mints for blocks around, every day after school. He honed his sales pitch on his long-suffering student mother and his mean sisters. It was amazing how many mints one could sell to suburban housewives simply by wearing pants with patches. Richard didn't have to phony up the look since iron-on patches were a staple in the Prosdocimi home in those lean years. The young merchant maxed out on mint sales, securing a spot in the full eight-week camp program. Millie was very proud of him, never realizing how he had pauperized the family to the surrounding community to the point that people would put an offering into the church basket for the family on Sundays.

The camp summer was an overall success for both Richard and Millie. While the son was earning merit badges, his mother finished her dissertation outline. What Richard did not get all summer long was a single good bag lunch from his mother. The rigors of graduate work did not allow Millie, despite her BS in home economics, enough time to think to buy Fritos or Twinkies for her son's lunch. An old banana or a liverwurst sandwich on heel bread does not cut it with an eight-year old boy, either now or then. As a consequence, Richard feigned the pauper again, repeatedly stuffing his unappealing lunch under the seat in deference to a passed tray to which everyone would contribute for him at lunchtime. If Millie had known what her son was doing to fill in for her motherly failures, she would have been mortified.

But none of this really hit Millie's radar screen. She was slicing through her graduate program as quickly as possible. She had earned a reputation in the department as a bright light, and she was making headway on her research on group dynamics in education. The kids were thriving even if they squabbled with each other constantly. There was one incident when the milkman tried to charge her for a dozen doughnuts each week (she never did notice the powdered sugar around Richard's mouth), but that passed without incident as she was astute enough and honest enough to pay for the doughnuts. Life was good. They had made it through 1962, and the summer of 1963 was fast approaching.

During her graduate years, Millie dragged the children to Ithaca once or twice a year to see family. This required a ten-hour car ride that was usually split over two days with an overnight stay at a Howard Johnson's in Indiana or Ohio along Route 80. Three children and a single student mother in an un-air-conditioned Oldsmobile for two days could provide material for a book by itself. Ithaca was worth it, however. Family, barbecues, fireflies, Purity ice cream, and swimming in the lake and creeks made for an idyllic time. During these visits, DoDo would always ask Millie when she was moving back to Ithaca. She didn't have the heart to tell him that would never happen.

That summer of 1963, Millie's older brother John hit the 5/10 at Caliente Racetrack in Tijuana for $63,000. He drove his new car back to Ithaca as the returning prodigal son. It was there and then that he and Millie cooked up the idea that Richard should travel back to California with John and his wife Kitty in order to spend some time with his father. Millie spoke to Andre and, amazingly, he bought into the idea.

In late July, Richard left Madison seated between John and Kitty in the front seat of a late-model Buick with no seat belts. By the time they reached Iowa, he had thrown up strawberry soda all over himself and the front seat. By Las Vegas, John understood why he had never had children. He and Kitty just left Richard alone in the seventeen-dollar-per-night motel for a few hours so they could play the slot machines. Who knew the nine year old would develop a severe ear infection that night and be delirious when they returned to the motel? John and Kitty did what any navy veteran couple would do in the situation, bundling him up in the backseat and driving through the night to get him to the nearest naval hospital—in San Diego. By then, the ear infection had blossomed into mastoids, but it was nothing that a course of powerful antibiotics and three or four days in the hospital couldn't fix.

Andre was at his bedside when Richard awoke in the hospital. He had driven down to San Diego from Santa Barbara, and he had brought a friend who he introduced as Shirley. When he came back in three days to drive Richard to his home, he came alone. On the ride north in his new Cadillac, he explained to Richard that Shirley was his wife and that they had two daughters named Diane and Sondra. This was a lot for Richard, so he just absorbed it and went with the flow.

During the next few weeks, as Richard recuperated, he got to know Shirley and the little girls (then three and one and a half) as well as a boy of ten can under the circumstances. He didn't see much of Andre since he seemed to always be at work. His one clear recollection of that month in Santa Barbara was being told every night that he needed to shower before bed. This was a big adjustment for a Midwestern boy used to a weekly bath. The other memory was of the promise of a bicycle that never materialized.

Meanwhile, Millie was back in Madison with the girls, feeling very guilty but making great progress on her research. After being forced to stay in California longer than expected to avoid flying with a recovering set of ears, Richard rejoined Millie and his sisters in mid-September with some valuable life lessons:

- Never drink strawberry pop on a road trip.
- Never bet with your chief petty officer uncle about road distances.
- Never trust your distant father when he introduces his wife as his "friend."
- Never assume that people outside the Midwest (especially in California) think one bath a week is sufficient hygiene.
- Don't ever count on getting a new bicycle.
- Never be afraid to tell your mother you want to come home after an extended and traumatic absence.

In late September, just as life was returning to normal with all three children back in the house, Millie got the call that her father had been killed in a car accident. John Uher was seventy-five years old and was being driven to a funeral by his brother when Joseph suffered a heart attack and ran across the road into an oncoming car. He did not survive the crash and was buried in three days in the same cemetery he had visited for his friend's funeral. Millie made the trip to Ithaca alone, preferring to leave the children to begin the new school year. When she returned in a week, she explained to the kids that DoDo had left her some money that she would use to move them all to a nicer house.

When JFK was shot several weeks later, every child in America learned about death, funerals, and grief. As sad as the assassination and media coverage of it was, it actually helped the children better understand their grandfather's death and somehow put it into context. For Millie, it had been a difficult and stressful fall. She lost her father and her idol almost at the same time.

The one physical possession Millie brought back from Myers was John's old cigar box. As she glanced into the heavy box, her focus fell on an odd copper coin that was bigger than a modern Lincoln penny, but smaller than a nickel. It had a flying eagle on one side and the date 1857 near the edge.

Millie had no idea what it was and what it was worth, but it suggested to her that taking this box of old coins was something her father would want her to do. She took the box home to Madison, sat down with Richard, and gave him the task of sorting them all out. She had bought a numismatic book to help him with the task. He jumped into it and had quickly made a full written list of the coins, indicating their year of issue, denomination, metallic composition, grade (uncirculated, extra fine, fine, good, fair, poor), and estimated value according to the book. Richard tended to upgrade each coin a bit, so his value estimates were overstated, but nonetheless, the collection had many valuable coins, such as the four Flying Eagle Pennies (only issued for four years in the 1850s) and an old 1805 nickel. There were also many foreign coins from around the world, none more interesting than the Chinese ones with the square holes in the middle.

Millie bought Richard all the supplies to protect each coin in its own sleeve in a three-ring binder with plastic sleeve holders. He put the valuation list in the back of the binder and then every year scratched out the value when the new book of values was issued. They changed only a bit each year, but Richard could see the value appreciation taking place before his eyes. Millie made him promise to always care for the coins and one day give them to his son as a remembrance of DoDo.

In 1964, while Millie was wrapping up her oral arguments on her dissertation, an odd thing happened. Andre sent her a legal notice that he had changed his name from Prosdocimi to Marin, which was his mother's maiden name. He was living in Santa Barbara and simply found the name Prosdocimi unworkable. The name Marin had all sorts of positive California connotations—not the least of which was the connection to the wealthy county north of San Francisco. This legal notice explained that to ensure proper legal rights for estate purposes, it would be advisable that she change her and the children's last name to Marin. With little hesitation, she filed for the name change, figuring it was the least she could do for her children's future.

This change coincided with the move from Madison to Middleton, an adjoining suburb—another fresh start of sorts. The family now had a new house, a new name, and practically a new identity since the schools were different and new friends entered their lives. Millie also transitioned from graduate student to postdoctoral fellow with the awarding of her PhD. Dr. Ludmilla Ann Marin, the diploma read. She was strangely proud of the fact that her bachelor's said Ludmilla Ann Uher, her master's diploma said Ludmilla Ann Prosdocimi, and now her latest diploma carried this third appellation.

Millie in front of her new Middleton home

As the newly christened Marin family settled into its new house, a new world opened up to them. They had a view of the lake and could watch the ice fishermen come and go to their warming huts. It had a secluded and wooded yard that showed off the seasons, especially autumn. The schools were more "professional." All three children attended a separate middle school (Kathy in eighth grade and Barbara and Richard in sixth). At school, Richard became seriously enamored with chemistry, so much so that he had his own amateur chem lab in his room. It was that lab and its Bunsen burner that almost burned down the new Marin residence.

Millie always had a way with figures of authority. She could talk her way out of traffic tickets, and on the occasion of this accidental fire, she managed to talk her way out of a bad report from the fire chief, who suspected that Richard's Bunsen burner was the cause of the fire. However, the chief also determined that the wiring was old and could have been the cause. This fire too was a sign. It required a refreshing of the whole house, paid for by insurance company money. All of this occurred at just the time when Millie was preparing to move on from academia.

Some people from AVCO Corporation, which had just become the recipient of a major Great Society contract to build and operate the first women's Job Corps Center in America, had noticed her resume. They had found a retired military man, Colonel Sol Ernst, to lead the effort, but they desperately needed a professional woman experienced and mature enough to take on the assignment as deputy and become the primary in-residence driver of the program.

Millie was flown to Washington DC and interviewed. Her stellar recommendations from NYS Welfare, the Rockefeller Foundation, ITDA, and the University of Wisconsin reinforced the sense of these buttoned-down businessmen that Millie was their person (despite having to drag around a bunch of teenagers in her wake). The program had been designated to be set up in rural South-Central Maine, a state with a desperate need for additional employment opportunities. Colonel Ernst would live in Portland and split his time between Washington and Maine. Millie's post was to be on the campus in Poland Spring, Maine, where young women were to be brought for life and vocational training. It was an interesting and ideal posting for Millie, playing perfectly to her administrative, educational, and developmental experience—as well as her chosen career direction.

The Badger State had been good to the family and had certainly prepared it for the Maine winters. Her new posting would give Millie the chance to get back on the slopes and teach the kids to ski. She even found herself wondering what Dave was up to and if he still skied in Vermont. The suburban experience was surely going to give way to a more rural existence in a new and somewhat raw place, but after what she had experienced, how underdeveloped could the state of Maine be?

125

CHAPTER 14

Snatchatory Rape
(Poland Spring, Maine, 1965–1968)

The Poland Spring house (circa 1965)

By January 1965, Millie and the kids were very used to moving whenever and wherever circumstances demanded. Other families delayed moves until the end of the school year, but that just wasn't a workable pattern moving north/south as they had. Why start bowing to a bureaucratically dictated school calendar when you can just barge in on the school year whenever needed?

A midyear move was one thing, but moving to Maine in the middle of a blizzard was quite another. To begin with, Maine could get ten feet of snow in the blink of an eye. The snowbanks from road plowing were so high that it was required to put a fluorescent Styrofoam ball on one's aerial in order to be sure to be seen approaching an intersection. And just such a ten-foot nor'easter blizzard was brewing that January. The state is called Vacationland—but not during blizzards.

Poland Spring was an old resort that was founded in the late eighteenth century, grew throughout the nineteenth, peaked in the roaring twenties, and had been in steady decline ever since. It was a large campus of several hundred acres that included three main residence buildings (the Poland Spring House, the new Poland Spring Inn, and the old Poland Spring Mansion House) as well as numerous other buildings such as a chapel, laundry, and administrative buildings. There was an eighteen-hole golf course (the first such course in the United States), several lakes with swimming and boating, a water-bottling plant (Poland Spring water has been famous since 1880 and is notable for its purity and absence of minerals), and—much to Millie's delight—a two thousand-foot ski area with T-bar lift and rope tow.

The Poland Spring House had a classic Victorian look like a seaside resort in Normandy or on the British coast. It boasted a center turret with matching wings extending out at a small angle like the prow of a proud ship. It had been a seasonal resort that shuttered itself in winter. While that would change compliments of Uncle Sam, in January 1965, it had the look and feel of a cross between the *Dr. Zhivago* Siberian Winter Palace and Jack Nicholson's hotel in *The Shining*.

The inn was much newer and stayed open for business during the winter. Millie and the children pulled up in their Chrysler New Yorker just as the storm was starting to howl. They parked the car, unloaded the necessities, and huddled in the warmth of the lobby fireplace as their rooms were readied. They would be staying at the inn for a few months until a house on the grounds was readied for them. The campus was strangely reminiscent of the grounds of the institute in Turrialba with its staff houses.

Halfway into the evening, Barbara suddenly realized that she had left her pet turtle in his plastic pond on the back window deck of the New Yorker. Looking out toward the parking lot and seeing nothing but feet of snow covering the cars and still coming down, Millie told Barbara there was nothing to be done that night. In the morning, the ten feet of snow was daunting even to the "Mainiacs" who regularly shoveled snow. It took two more days to uncover the New Yorker and retrieve the frozen solid turtle pond.

Millie explained to Barbara that all things die, and the little turtle certainly had gone peacefully as it froze to death several days ago. In order to give it a proper toilet burial, Millie ran the pond under the warm water tap for several minutes. To her complete surprise, the thawed turtle swam around in the sink as if nothing had happened. She could only wonder where it would have ended up if she had flushed it frozen. The family took this as a good omen that even a blizzard could not deter them from their destiny in Vacationland.

Millie's task that winter was to begin the planning for the entire Job Corps center. There was a great deal to be done in the nine months before opening. The program had been started by President Lyndon Johnson in the post-Camelot idealism of the mid-1960s. Sargent Shriver was running the Office of Economic Opportunity (OEO), and Job Corps was its flagship program, initiated in multiple formats to test their relative effectiveness. Millie's job was to set up a residency program of one- and two-year durations for 1,200 inner-city women aged sixteen through twenty-one. They would learn a valuable vocation and would also be taught the social skills deemed necessary to participate in middle-class American life, from personal hygiene to such far-reaching things as "polite" recreation.

Millie with several Job Corps students

As the program had been outsourced to AVCO Corporation, budgeting and efficiency were considered paramount since those factors would determine how much of future programs would be insourced or outsourced. The only novel aspect for Millie was the residency part. It was an aggressive social program, but it had strong social objectives. Millie liked the career challenge but always wondered how realistic it was to attempt to effect transformation of these young women in every aspect. The economic goals proved to be the easiest for her to achieve; the Poland Spring Center was the only one of 122 centers in the United States that met its budgetary objectives. Needless to say, AVCO would be quite pleased with the program

Millie with her AVCO colleagues

During that long first Maine winter, Richard and Barbara attended school two miles away at the Poland Community School. Kathy had to trek sixteen miles to her high school in Lewiston/Auburn. Maine was then ranked forty-ninth in the nation in education, a fact of which Millie was acutely aware. Coming in midyear to seventh grade from an enlightened system such as Wisconsin's posed no problem for Richard and Barbara. What was problematic was that, for the first time, they had no choice but to be in the same classroom. As cerebral as Richard tended to be,

129

Barbara was equally social and popular. Their differences made for many interesting interactions.

On weekends, the local school kids loved to come up to Poland Spring and go exploring on the grounds. This was a unique moment in the resort's history. It was now leased by the American government, but it really had not yet been taken over by the government as the planning was still underway. This made for some interesting exploratory outings for the kids. Wandering through the old hotel in the off-season was always a little spooky, but that year, the owners had allowed some sort of blowout party or last hurrah and didn't bother cleaning up after it. There were half-full champagne glasses, women's shoes, and miscellaneous artifacts strewn all over the place, and a good portion of winter dust covered everything. One of the reasons this lease made sense for the owners was because the hotel hadn't seen a lick of renovation or even maintenance for many years. In a word, the place was crumbling. There were hallways where the only thing holding the floor together seemed to be the carpet runner. The stairs up to the towers were particularly decrepit, and they were truly scary places with cobwebs and dead vermin all around.

The government was prepared to spend huge money to bring everything up to something like OSHA code, even though there was not yet an OSHA. The enormity of the physical plant challenges gave rise to tremendous local job opportunities for every imaginable skill set. It may well be that this local economic impact far exceeded the upward economic mobility created for the program participants. A fully staffed fire department was even created just for the center. The biggest beneficiary of all this improvement to the physical plant was WMTW television, the local channel housed in one of the Poland Spring outbuildings that used Mount Washington as its wide-range signal tower.

In addition to occasional visits from the likes of *Tonight Show* host Jack Paar, who owned a place in Maine, WMTW was best known for sending a goofy guy up to the summit weather station on Mount Washington to spend four months in isolation, broadcasting daily weather spots that got increasingly weird as his cabin fever progressed over the winter. This all added to the charm of the hilltop campus.

While Richard and the girls settled into the family's first house at the edge of campus and then their new house on the eighteenth hole of the golf course, Millie worked diligently to prepare for the arrival of the first class of students in September. The summer was spent mostly on the golf course (Richard grooved permanent notches into his shoulders from double bag caddying for five dollars per bag per loop). The girls spent the summer at the beach house at the lake, paddling around Upper Range Lake in the canoe Millie bought for them.

While Richard learned the ins and outs of locker room Acey-Deucy gambling (sometimes losing a whole day's wages in ten minutes), the girls built up a coterie of local friends and honed their domestic skills, most notably sewing. Richard got his golf handicap down to a fourteen, but Kathy topped that by excelling in the national Singer sewing competition, taking her velvet dress to the national finals. Millie stayed very busy on the hill, making Colonel Ernst look good to the bosses at AVCO.

When the center opened in September 1965, it employed 800 local and imported staff to work with the 1,200 students and maintain the 175-year-old buildings. The participants were about 60 percent African American, 20 percent Hispanic American, and 20 percent white. This mix was a challenge to the local community, which was more Appalachian than Nor'easter. But nothing was more challenging than the staff's job of dealing with more than a thousand displaced young ladies, far from home, out of their urban element, and removed from the men with whom they were used to socializing.

Realizing that expecting total abstinence from these young women was simply unrealistic, Millie cut a deal with the Acadia Air Force Base to ship in some able-bodied soldiers every week for general stress release. This had some expected consequences. The center was prepared for many medical needs, but perhaps not the inordinate number of childbirths, which often went hidden and undiagnosed, particularly with the larger girls. It was not unheard of for a student to arrive alone and leave with a new baby, despite all the sex education and contraception available.

Millie built up a full collection of switchblades, razor knives, and ice picks that were confiscated from students, several that she personally had to forcibly take from overly aggressive women. Many of the fights that broke out took place over the limited number of men available. On one occasion, Millie asked a favorite student of hers how her relationship with Leroy was going. The earnest young woman sneered and said, "I'm not with Leroy no more. If I were, they would arrest me for snatchatory rape." Millie told her children that story over dinner, thinking it a perfect descriptor of how much her students were learning about life, but at the same time, the distance still to go to get them fully up to speed.

Life on the campus of Poland Spring was idyllic all year. The Job Corps women were given the opportunity to learn new sports like skiing, archery, and even roller-skating (in the old grand ballroom), perhaps reflecting the overreach in terms of social transformation goals. Meanwhile, Millie and the kids were in a wonderful Vacationland that afforded lots of recreational experiences. Everyone learned to ski on the small upside-down ski area (one where the ski lodge was at the top of the hill rather than the bottom), where Richard also learned the virtues of busing dishes in the lodge in exchange for a season skiing pass. The fifty-dollar price tag of the pass equated to an hourly wage of about $0.30, well below the minimum wage of $1.10—a quick lesson for Richard in bad negotiating.

Millie took the children on ski trips into her old haunts in New Hampshire and Vermont. On one such trip, she left them for an evening to visit an old friend at Sugarbush Lodge. She never mentioned the friend's name, just telling them that it was an old skiing buddy of hers. She had gone to meet Dave—but not to rekindle anything other than shared fond memories. In the years since their acquaintance, he had become extremely prominent in New York legal and financial circles and even taken a spot as a Cornell trustee. Millie returned to the lodge a bit misty, but no worse for wear and ready for another day on the slopes with the kids on the "blue ice" of Cannon Mountain in Franconia Notch, New Hampshire.

In the spring of 1967, with the Job Corps program in full swing and the people at AVCO feeling good about their fledging effort in the world of OEO work, Millie began to worry about Richard's education. The school in Poland, Maine, was simply lacking in rigor—not to mention cultural opportunities. Therefore, she decided to send him away to prep school, settling on nearby Hebron Academy. Kathy would continue in Lewiston/Auburn high school, and Barbara (far more concerned about her friends and staying connected than about academics) would join her there. Richard, meanwhile, left to spend a year in pursuit of a classical education with Latin and literature at its core and athletics in every season, surrounded by only men and boys. Millie had always fretted that she had failed to provide Richard with sufficient male exposure. What she didn't realize was that there were few male role models more masculine, independent, and testosterone-prone than the adventurous and athletic role model she herself presented.

One particular episode dramatically demonstrated this fact. One day in the summer of 1967, while Richard was in the house packing to head off to Hebron, Millie was outside in the yard when a large, local bully of a dog named Sam, half-shepherd and half-wolf, wandered into the yard. The small family dog, Puddles, was half-Labrador and half-miniature collie. Sam did not like Puddles and certainly did not respect any territorial boundaries Puddles might try to set, so they went at it with Sam in distinct advantage. Richard looked out the window in wonder as Millie took her broom and fearlessly entered the fray, slamming Sam in the head until he released Puddles's neck from his jaws. She yelled at Sam and chased him away. Richard, by now a strapping fourteen-year old, was himself scared to death of Sam. It made quite a notable impression on him to see his mother combatively mix it up with this half-wolf in defense of the family mutt. Millie looked at Puddles's wounds, determined they were minor, and went on about her chores as though nothing had happened. Richard just stared at the scene in wonder and respect for his Mater Gladiatrix.

While Richard was away at Hebron learning the classics and the finer points of manhood, Millie began to realize that the Job Corps probably had a finite lifecycle, despite the good work it was doing. She traveled to Washington D.C. to meet with the AVCO brass, where she was showered with praise for her budgetary success. They didn't give a damn about the programmatic success, she realized. Even though they were anxious to have a successful woman like Millie in their ranks and offered her many ideas for next assignments, she decided that she had run her course with AVCO just as the Great Society was running its course with the American political system. Upon leaving Poland Spring, her first stop (yes, it was Dave's suggestion) was Cornell.

At that time, Cornell's Home Economics School was repositioning itself into a School of Human Ecology to shed its old-time "housewife" image. Again, many of her former teachers very much wanted Millie to join the faculty as an associate professor. She considered the opportunity with a particular eye toward the free tuition plan—particularly attractive to a woman with three teenage children needing higher education. She insisted on a full-tenured professorship based on her life experience, and that might well have been forthcoming. As the university ground its gears over this counteroffer, however, the United Nations came calling.

It is unclear how the UN had heard about Millie, but she suspected it was some combination of Joe DiFranco, her senior professors at Wisconsin, and some at OEO who felt her talents were wasted at AVCO ... or maybe it was Dave again. In any case, the UN offer was for a post at the Food and Agriculture Organization located in Rome. The position was designated as what was called a P-5, without diplomatic status. Millie hung tough, however. She told them she would only consider it with the higher D-1 designation, signifying full diplomatic status. Unlike Cornell, which was still wrangling over her counterproposal, FAO immediately agreed and signed her up. She went through the motions of a family discussion about the move, but the kids were so ingrained in the move-along program that they knew the relocation was a foregone conclusion. They were also mightily intrigued with Rome as a destination, which made for an easy unanimous vote (Barbara actually abstained due to social conflicts of interest).

In the summer of 1968, therefore, the Marin family headed to New York City to catch the SS *Michelangelo* of the Italian Line from pier 80 for Naples, Italy. While in New York City, Millie showed her wide-eyed children all the sights and made a visit to the lobby of Rockefeller Center for old times' sake. The kids were especially impressed with how much Millie knew about the lobby frescoes, as Dave had been many years before.

After boarding the ship for Italy, they stood on the starboard deck to salute Lady Liberty as they steamed out of the harbor and under the recently completed Verrazano-Narrows Bridge at the mouth of the harbor. The voyage would take seven days, and the kids would have the run of the ship. Because Puddles was in the kennel, the whole family was given entree to first class since it was assumed anyone silly enough to take a dog on an ocean liner would be traveling first class.

Although Richard was still sharing a stateroom (and bunk) with Millie, the access to liberal bartenders and lots of kids returning to school in Rome made the trip very interesting. On the last night of the crossing, after passing through the Straits of Gibraltar at dusk, Richard made the mistake of staying out all night with the gang. In the wee morning hours before docking in Naples, Millie had her first experience with disciplining her young man. He already towered over her by seven or eight inches, so when she grabbed his jaw to smell if he had been drinking (he had), she found that a swift slap to his face was blocked by him for the first time in their parent-child relationship. Millie took this in stride, glaring at him, and told him to get ready to depart. She was secretly glad, however, that he was respectfully showing the backbone she hoped he would show throughout his life.

CHAPTER 15

Circus Maximus
(Rome, Italy, 1968–1975)

Dr. Ludmilla A. Marin FAO/UN diplomat

The Marin family's arrival in Naples was nothing short of classic Italian. Leaving the port, there were throngs of cars trying to jam through one small exit—with no lanes and no sense of priority or decorum. It was every driver for himself with no apparent rule of law. The taxi driver clarified that the one law every Italian knew, and which was enforced, was that any pedestrian hit and killed in a crosswalk was entitled to a burial at the expense of the offending driver. This was a good thing since Italy at the time did not have mandatory liability insurance coverage. So driving in Italy in the sixties was more or less like the American Wild West.

The family saw many more eye-opening roadside events during the two-hour trip to Rome's southern suburb, called EUR, where they would be living for at least the next few months. The neighborhood was at the end of the one and only metro line in Rome. It seems that every time someone had tried to expand the metro system, they had run into an archaeological site and had to halt work. The only reason the single line to EUR had been built was that Mussolini had damned the archeologists and said full steam ahead to his new model city of EUR, which was intended to be a symbol of his new order. The old adage that at least Mussolini made the trains run on time held some truth to it.

One of the first things the family did was take the metro to the Circo Massimo stop (in between the Pyramide Cestia and the Colloseo stations). This brought them to the base of the Aventine Hill, one of the fabled Seven Hills of Rome (think Buster Keaton in *A Funny Thing Happened on the Way to the Forum*) and at the Circus Maximus (think chariot races). In keeping with the grandeur of Rome, another thing Mussolini had built were many grand government offices. One such building sprawled across the lower Aventine Hill adjacent to the Baths of Caracalla. This was destined to be the Ministry of Ethiopian Affairs (strangely enough, the place presumably where Silvano Prosdocimi Sr. would have held court), but after the war, the building had become the headquarters for the UN's Food and Agriculture Organization (FAO). The motto of FAO is "Fiat Panis," the Latin phrase for "Let there be bread" in keeping with the book of Genesis, with its proclamation of "Fiat Lux" ("Let there be light")—or perhaps Giovanni Agnelli's Fiat ("Let there be cars").

The purpose of the visit, besides Millie formally reporting for duty, was to show the teens how to get to her place of work and the FAO commissary, the font of all otherwise impossible-to-find groceries of American origin. This was also where one got one's ration of gas coupons. Gasoline was five hundred lira per liter or $3.15 per gallon, versus $0.34 per gallon in the United States. However, the most important event of the visit was that the whole family was photographed for their CD cards. These were the Italian Corpo Diplomatico ID cards that were essentially "Get out of jail for free" cards—or at very least, "Don't give me that traffic ticket, officer" cards. To Millie, who already had her Laissez Passer or UN diplomatic passport, this was no big deal, but to three teenagers thinking about all

137

the possibilities this might afford, it was a very big deal. Millie was not so worried about Kathy, but she sensed that Barbara's social instincts and Richard's mischievous nature might make them fall prey to this temptation. The metro ride home was given over to a lecture about not abusing the CD cards.

The woman Millie was replacing was Jane Ebbs, a retired army colonel who had been on the job for five years. A Texan, she was effusive in welcoming the new arrivals from Stateside and invited them to dinner at her Aventine apartment. While they were there, she noticed Richard looking at her amphora antiquities. She asked if he like archaeology—a great icebreaker for someone who had boxes of old dusty pre-Colombian relics among the family's shipped (and currently en route) belongings. Jane went on to explain that one could not just pick up rocks or souvenirs in the Forum or other sites around Rome, but that there was another great spot for collectors.

The explanation was that in Phoenician days—when the Tiber River was navigable—the ships would come up the river to the City and dock at the first big bend near the Pyramide Cestia. The boats would unload their goods with all the amphorae that carried grains and oils stored in casks for easier cart transport. For sanitary purposes, the laws of Rome forbade the reuse of amphorae (think "No deposit, no return") so shippers discarded the amphorae by the riverbank. Over the centuries, they accumulated there to form Testaccio Hill (*Testae* in Latin means *shards*), a large trash heap of discarded amphorae. Richard's project for the next day became digging for and gathering as many handles, jug necks, and shards with markings that he could carry. This box would sit for years in Millie's home, close to the dusty pre-Colombian artifact boxes (right next to the old cigar box and coin collection.). In 1969, Testaccio Hill was declared a national historic site—and no more digging for antiquities was allowed thereafter. But the salvage law of the seas prevailed, with both Millie and Richard benefiting as in the old adage: "finders, keepers."

Before embarking on her assignment at FAO, Millie finalized the kids' schooling, which she had mostly prepared in advance of arriving. Kathy and Barbara were to go to Marymount School for Girls, and Richard would go to Notre Dame International Prep for Boys. It was interesting and not unnoticed by all members of the Marin family that these naturalized

Presbyterians were now being forced to revert to their Catholic roots. Having been baptized Catholics, the three children somehow made the Sisters of Marymount and the Brothers of the Holy Cross feel that they had a chance to redeem their young souls. Nevertheless, Millie registered them as non-Catholics, which meant they would take ethics classes instead of catechism.

As Millie made her way around the bureaucracy that was FAO, she met many like-minded developmentalists and educationalists—as well as every variety of food scientists, nutritionists, forestry and fishery specialists, and agronomists. She was technically the Chief of the Home Economics Service of the Nutrition Division, which made her the highest-ranking woman at FAO in 1968 and the first to attain diplomatic status. While that worked well for her organizationally, it was clearly a major point of contention among the professional men who had worked at FAO for years and had not had the nerve to negotiate as hard as a Millie had done coming in. What it meant in addition to status and CD cards was a bit more money and a much bigger office with a rug. Apparently, a rug was a major status symbol in the 1968 FAO hierarchy.

The two people to whom Millie gravitated most readily were a Dutch-Canadian food scientist named Edward Asselbergs and a Texas woman named Frankie Hansell. Both had been in FAO for some time. Ed was in a different division, but he had a passel of kids with ages that more or less matched the ages of Millie's gang. Frankie was a nutritionist in Millie's division with lots of moxie and an outgoing manner.

The family was invited out to the Asselbergs' home in a distant suburb halfway to the beach in Ostia Lido. The suburb, Casal Palocco, had clearly been modeled on American planned suburbs, including trees and sidewalks. This seemed somehow appropriate since Ed had the distinction of being the food scientist who had invented and patented instant mashed potatoes, a symbolic staple of suburban American life at that time. The Asselbergs had five children who spanned the ages of ten to eighteen, all of whom went to Marymount or Notre Dame. All were slender enough to wonder if they ever ate any instant mashed potatoes.

Bobby Asselbergs, who was Richard's age (fourteen going on forty), became his best friend for the duration of his high school career at Notre Dame. The two had met during the family's visit to Casal Palocco. Out of politeness, Bobby had been asked to show Richard around while his sisters hung with Kathy and Barbara and Millie chatted with Ed and his wife.

Bobby's first comment to Richard was that he had a scooter, followed by a question as to whether Richard was going to get one. It would be untrue to say that Richard had never noticed the hordes of scooters and mopeds on the streets of Rome or wondered about riding one. Bobby ended up selling Richard his Lambretta 50 cc scooter with Millie's consent—consistent with her view that boys needed to morph into men on their own. Bobby's motive in selling was to buy a faster motorbike.

While Bobby was able to race circles around Richard on his newly purchased red Ducati 50 cc, two-stroke motorbike, Richard carefully putted along, trying not to fall off or get knocked off too often. Bobby, a young motorcycle zealot, was all too happy to teach Richard about them by getting him to buy the latest motorcycle magazines (naturally, for joint consumption) and having Richard use his bountiful supply of gas coupons for both of them. Since Millie didn't have a car yet, Richard had a virtually limitless supply.

Bobby taught Richard many things. Having lived in Rome for a dozen years, he spoke Italian fluently and was able to teach Richard all the major swear word categories. Since they attended the same school, they drove back and forth to school together or took the same bus. Streetwise Bobby showed Richard what was what in Rome, including where all the campfire girls (ladies of the evening) hung out and how much they cost. They had a lot of fun stopping to chat with the occasional pretty one only to have Bobby ask for a student discount and race off, leaving Richard to sheepishly contend with an awkward exit.

The Asselbergs were a big family. Bobby had two brothers and two sisters, and he was smack in the middle. His parents were Canadians by way of immigration from Holland and were now in Rome for the duration. When the two boys hung out at Bobby's house, there were always chores to be done. One regular chore was washing Ed's pride and joy: his new silver Mercedes sedan. While they were washing, Ed would stand there and shout orders if they missed a spot. Though he was always pleasant enough to Richard, the boy sensed that Ed was sore at him for some unexplained reason. Years later, Richard learned from

Millie that Ed's resentment had sprung from the fact that she had been brought in with diplomatic status while he had worked for years at FAO to achieve his. Whatever the reason, Ed seemed a tough dude—and Richard generally steered clear of him.

Lunchtime at Bobby's house usually consisted of soup. He always encouraged Richard to stay for lunch since, on those occasions, his mother would fry croutons in butter to put in the soup. The skinny Asselbergs kids ate that soup and relished those croutons as if it were a seven-course dinner. They then happily went out to wash and wax Dad's car again. Bobby did odd jobs for pocket money, and between that and what Richard had to spare, the boys pretty much had their run of the town.

Just about everything Richard learned about motorcycle mechanics, he learned from Bobby. They would fieldstrip either of their bikes and do virtually anything and everything that needed doing. This was relatively easy since both bikes had two-stroke engines—that is, they had no valves and lubricated themselves through a combination of the oil sump and the "miscela" gasoline they used. This was an oil and gas mixture that was pumped in combination at gas stations. Two-strokes were common enough so that every station had such a pump. The process began with hand-pumping a preset amount of oil into a Plexiglas chamber and then filling it the rest of the way with gas. The high-pitched whine of the two-stroke engine revving at ten thousand rpms or more sounded like a sewing machine on a cocktail of steroids and speed.

Everything the boys did had to do with motorcycles—from wheelies to running bump-starts. One day, Bobby said he wanted to buy an even bigger bike. About to turn sixteen, he was eligible for a motorcycle license. He had his eye on a used bike and wanted to sell Richard his Ducati—that is, if Richard thought he could handle it! Bobby helped Richard find a buyer for his scooter, and they worked out a deal worthy of the most sophisticated Wall Street financier, involving both cash and paper (the prized gas coupons). Richard proudly concluded the transaction without parental involvement, announcing to Millie what he had done. She just looked at him and shook her head. It was hard to say if that was disapproval for the deal Richard had cut or for his not telling her about the transaction in advance or her disappointment because she had hoped Richard would outgrow motorcycles. Whatever it meant, it took the edge off Richard's deal-doing pride, even if not off his pleasure of owning a piece of the world of Ducati.

While Richard was messing with motorbikes, Kathy and Barbara spent a year going to Marymount every day in their Catholic girls' school uniforms, complete with navy blue pleated skirts and knee socks. The program involved waiting for the bus in EUR near one of the many bars (in Italy, serving both alcohol and coffee). Neither Kathy nor Barbara liked being under the thumb of the Marymount nuns. Kathy was anxious to leave for college to study architecture, and Barbara found the social stifling of the nuns inconsistent with her personal social goals. Before long, they had both solved their problem. Kathy was admitted to Washington University's Architecture School, and Barbara began dating a rock band lead singer and then insisted that she be allowed to transfer to the Overseas School of Rome. Millie had many mixed feelings about the former and minimal concerns about the latter. No mother wants her daughter to go down wild and uncertain paths. It's hard to say if Millie held a double standard for her children on how much wild and crazy they should have. It was more likely that she individualized her concerns rather than "genderizing" them. Washington University was in Saint Louis, and OSR was on the Via Cassia and was occupied by all the cool teenagers of Rome.

Barbara's boyfriend Tony and his rock band, the Free Love, were the hottest ticket in Italy and maybe Europe. By dating him, she gained instant notoriety in the Roman teenage pantheon of cool. In contrast, Richard ran in a completely different less-than-cool orbit of bikers. Kathy basically eschewed cool at all costs as a matter of principle.

With her children charting their own respective and quite different paths, Millie was free to settle in at FAO. This was her power moment. She was fifty-two years old and as much in charge as any woman in the UN world. But before she could dig in, she had to take care of one piece of personal business. When Andre had heard of Millie's new posting, he had called her to ask a favor. By then, he had moved on from his second wife, Shirley, and their two girls, Diane and Sondra, had misfired on another marriage in California, and had skipped town to Mexico City where he was courting the daughter of one of the landed conquistadores' families and building the new Camino Real Hotel for his California development company. He was feeling the need for a prestige boost and had asked Millie to get him a parchment diploma from the University of Padua. evidencing his graduation from the architecture program there in 1944. He swore he had earned the degree, but that the war had disrupted his graduation. Millie knew better than either to believe or question this fantasy.

She never understood what Svengali power he held over her. Millie was a realist with her feet on the ground, but it was simply impossible for her to say no to Andre. So she ventured into the back alleys of Rome to find an experienced forger of considerable note, who was able to produce an elaborate illuminated diploma that looked like a medieval manuscript. A thing of beauty, it cost Millie as much as several years' tuition in prewar Padua would have cost. When the old bohemian gentleman delivered the rolled diploma to her, he treated it like a great master, but he pointed out to her that Padua did not even graduate a class in 1944—compliments of Mussolini's followers. Millie knew that Andre would be unbothered by such a trivial detail.

At work, Millie began with a thorough review of all the worldwide programs under her control. It was this review that introduced her to Frankie Hansell, who had set up and run programs in India, Ceylon, Nepal, the Philippines, Cambodia, Pakistan, Laos, Indonesia, and Thailand. Given that FAO's portfolio was concentrated in Asia, Africa, and Latin America, Millie saw great value in someone as competent and familiar with Asia as Frankie was. Millie's existing knowledge of Latin America was secure, so with Frankie by her side, she needed only an Africa specialist—and then she would be comfortable reaching for local expertise whenever and wherever she needed.

Over lunch with Frankie to discuss her elevation to deputy status, Millie mentioned her old friend Joe DiFranco in Costa Rica, of whom she had long since lost track. Frankie stopped her on the spot and explained that Dr. Joseph DiFranco had been in the Program Division of FAO for several years.

Millie and her female staff

Millie postponed her search for an Africa specialist and immediately dropped everything to seek out her old friend Joe. When she walked into his rugless office in a different part of the FAO complex, he was less surprised than she thought. After giving her a big hug, he explained that he had heard she was coming and decided to wait and see how long it would take her to find him. They spent much of the afternoon catching up on family and career activities and talking a bit about the politics of FAO. He told Millie that the Dutchman who was currently the director general was a lot like their former Dutch fearless leader from Costa Rica. Bigger organization, more resources, broader field of play—same old game.

Marjorie was positively in her element in Rome. Millie had never seen her so happy. Marjorie had found a lovely little apartment on the Janiculum Hill, looking east over the dusky cityscape of Rome, and the home was as comfortable and inviting as ever. Her gracious welcome to Millie and the kids made them all feel wonderful. There was an undertone of melancholy to Marjorie, however, despite the pleasant setting. Millie suspected that it had to do with her having to leave her daughter Mindy back in San Jose with her new husband. Marjorie was showing the signs of too much global travel for a suburban American housewife. Joe only had three years to go till retirement, and Millie figured it was none too soon for her old friends.

As the Marins were leaving after dinner, Joe told Millie that he had an idea concerning a possible African specialist for her office. When she called him to follow up the next morning, he explained that he had met a young woman from Kansas who had done good work in Nigeria and Malawi. She was young, but she was already very respected for her work in country. As a reflection of the generally suspicious view of Americans in FAO, they were significantly underrepresented in the agency, compared to the nation's financial contribution. Millie had a unit that was largely staffed by non-Americans, however, so she had some leeway to hire another staffer from the United States. Accordingly, she reached out to Natalie Hahn of Kansas to probe her interest in coming to Rome.

Natalie was a unique young woman who reminded Millie of her own daughter Kathy. She was smart, serious, and headstrong, and she had a passion for Africa, which is what Millie needed. Millie broke with tradition by hiring a person who hadn't yet done her graduate work, though Natalie would not disappoint her—earning her EdD at Harvard only a few years later.

Once Millie got her area organized and her arms around the gist of the programmatic initiatives in her unit, she felt it was time to hit the road. She had done some traveling during her first year, but she was ready to go out and have some meaningful impact. Kathy was in college, and Barbara and Richard seemed sufficiently settled in to take care of themselves. She planned to put Richard in charge of paying the bills and administering the finances of the household and asked Barbara to manage the domestic issues like food and the weekly housekeeping. This arrangement reflected Millie's firm belief that responsibility was the key to growth.

During Barbara and Richard's junior and senior years in high school, Millie spent perhaps six of each twelve months in the field in one- or two-month intervals. It never quite seemed enough from a work perspective to Millie. She believed that her presence was a key motivational ingredient for her services' program success. But she was also a conscientious parent who realized that she only had a few more years to shape her two remaining chicks. She felt they each needed her in their own way. Barbara, the gentle social soul, needed to know she was worthy of love and that she had much due her. Barbara gave and gave in relationships, and in the process, she did everything a mother does not want her daughter to do … twice. Richard just needed to have his wild side controlled so he could let his academic side flourish. A good student, he was always precariously balanced on the edge. If he could stay upright, his mind would carry him through.

Millie with her male FAO peers

Millie was most often the only senior woman in the room at symposia and plenary gatherings, but women officers dominated the field. It always bothered Millie that the ground-level people who did so much of the good work were unable to rise naturally in the organization. It was an extension of the double standard that existed in many of the developing nations of the world. Women were allowed to work hard, but they were not allowed to own and hold property or make important decisions. Women were the key to ground-level development on both sides of the operation, but they were not positioned to lead. Millie took this as a personal challenge, given her unusually elevated position at FAO. She viewed it as an obligation to the women working in development and the women in need of change in the developing world to be their champion. Yet she never wore the mantle well. Her Old World side thought that women simply needed to do the work and make smart educational and career decisions. She always fought for them to be given equal opportunity, but never to be handed power or position for its own sake or in order to correct past injustice.

It should have pained Millie privately to put her son in charge of the property and her daughter in charge of the housework when she left for the field to advocate for women all around the world, she felt the need. But this irony apparently never occurred to her. One was theory and macro, and the other was reality and pragmatically micro. Had someone pointed it out to her as hypocritical, she would have looked at them with tilted head, shrugged, and moved on. Reality and theory were purposefully separate arenas.

At the end of a monthlong trip, she arrived home to Richard with a recovering sore throat and Barbara off for the night with Tony of the Free Love. Richard mentioned that he had stayed home from school that day, but he showed her a paper he had written on Friedrich Nietzsche and his view on Ars Gratia Artis by Gautier (for his ethics course). The next day, Brother John, the disciplinary dean at Notre Dame, was displeased that Richard did not bring an absentee note as was required; he had forgotten to ask Millie to write one. Brother John called Millie at work with Richard sitting in front of him, appealing to her as an educationalist and manager. As Richard watched Brother John's face distort, he sensed the call was not going as planned. This was confirmed when Brother John said, "And exactly what rules do you think are stupid, Dr. Marin?" The call ended shortly thereafter, and Brother John just waved Richard out of the room.

Millie cared about results, not rules—and certainly not convention.

CHAPTER 16

Via Baccina
(Rome, Italy, 1975–1980)

Via Baccina in Rome

Once Barbara and Richard went off to college (Barbara to join Kathy at Washington University in Saint Louis and Richard to Millie's alma mater, Cornell University in Ithaca), Millie rethought her Roman existence. The family had lived for three years in a large penthouse in suburban EUR, which seemed right for the family. Now that the nest had emptied, Millie allowed herself new freedom. Having always wanted to live the artist's lifestyle in a garret in the old city, she sold off most of her furniture and took a fifth-floor walk-up on Via Baccina. Her new street was wedged between the Coliseum and the highly commercial Via Cavour on the Esquiline Hill of Rome. The end of the street to the west dead-ended in the Forum of Caesar, in pretty much the center of the old city of Rome. Her apartment had a small center courtyard open to the sky, surrounded by sloped ceiling rooms with small low windows. This was the real deal: a traditional garret apartment, a small, intimate space with lots of charm and very steep stairs.

While it was technically a two-bedroom apartment, Millie did not expect any of her chicks to return to the nest. In her new space, she had no choice but to default to the traditional Roman lifestyle of shopping daily for food. The refrigerator was small, and the storage space for any staples was nearly nonexistent. Of necessity, her shopping was done at small shops on Via Baccina. During the seven years she lived in Rome, she had never bothered to learn Italian. Perhaps because Barbara and Richard spoke decent Italian, she had found no need. All of her work was in English. Her Spanish was excellent, and it was a serviceable day-to-day language for her. She spoke Spanish to the merchants, and they understood her and spoke back to her in Italian, which she understood. Practical and effective, though not textbook—just like Millie.

Just as the kids went off to school in 1975, Millie was in the middle of organizing the first International Women's Year gathering in Mexico City. With all the bra burning in the sixties, it is interesting that it took until 1975 for women's organizations and feminist leaders to gather their forces sufficiently to organize a meeting to discuss advancing their collective cause globally. Her attendance at the conference gave Millie an opportunity to travel up to New York City afterward.

Millie always made sure to visit the UN mother ship in New York City whenever she was in the hemisphere, but this time, her itinerary also included Saint Louis (to see Kathy and Barb), Ithaca (to check in on Richard and the Uher clan), and New York City. All seemed well on all fronts. Her general view, based mostly on her own life journey, was to assume that once in college, the kids were on their own, at least in terms of self-determination and direction. She never questioned any of the three about their choice of curriculum or their academic performance. She assumed this was best and was what they all wanted. She was perhaps two-thirds right.

While Kathy and Richard wended their way through their higher education, Barbara was less clear in her direction. She bounced around among a few different schools and programs until Millie broke her own rules of disengagement and suggested that she come home to Rome. While this was ostensibly so that Millie could help Barbara sort out her direction in life, at fifty-seven years old, she was also in need of some support. Millie and Barbara forged a bond that would remain strong for the next forty-plus years. Millie helped her daughter settle down, and Barbara helped run her mother's hectic professional life.

At FAO, Millie had been promoted to the position of director. Given the mandatory retirement age of sixty-two, it was unlikely that Millie would ever rise any higher in the organization. When one gets to that career stage, of course, it's a difficult moment. If one is as driven as Millie had been for forty years, it's an even more dramatic time. The iconic *60 Minutes* anchor Harry Reasoner once did a bit where he described the phenomenon of career ambition over time, describing the impact of reaching the age of sixty. He likened it to an epiphany where one can finally feel at peace with oneself. The demons that drove Millie did indeed seem to find peace at that point in her career. She had flown her freak flag enough and climbed enough Via Baccina stairs, so that as soon as Barbara recommended it, she moved back out to EUR to a pleasant two-bedroom house. Barbara helped her entertain more regularly and basically enjoy her rank and privilege, as well deserved as it was.

The problem with development work is that it never ends since the problems are never permanently fixed. Ironically, one of the countries that was considered developmentally "fixed" was Costa Rica. It had a long-running democracy and a stable, though small economic foundation that broadened its middle class and gave it the best profile of any Central American economy. Venezuela was also considered to have shifted to the ranks of developed nations. This was best exemplified by its membership in OPEC, which in some ways qualified it as super-developed and a notch better than oil-consuming Western powers.

Aside from a few nations such as Costa Rica and Venezuela that the UN regarded as exceptions that had crossed into developed status, regional development in the rest of the world seemed a bottomless pit for efforts and resources. Nothing Millie could possibly do would ever move the needle in Africa, for example, where tribalism still ran rampant—and the early stages of climate change were turning whole swaths of heretofore productive farmland into bone-dry desert. Southeast Asia was also a complete conundrum. As the Asian Tigers got claws and began to roar, the rest of the nations in the region were sinking further and further into despair. Nowhere exemplified this more than India, where education had taken root from the colonial heritage, but cultural stratification (the caste system) and sheer population numbers made progress always seem trivial compared to the growing problems. This was particularly the case with respect to the backward status of women all across India, especially in the rural areas where girls were intentionally left uneducated to keep them in their place.

Millie cared enough to work hard on problems and to not overthink the endgame. She had begun in development work in 1937. Forty years later, much had been accomplished, yet much remained to be done. Millie managed to put this in perspective as she set her program plans into motion. She had helped young professionals like Natalie establish themselves for the future while tapping the experience of seasoned pros like Frankie. She preferred getting things done to building a legacy, believing that the sign of true success was putting in place a team that could eclipse the success that she herself had achieved.

While Millie was setting up her endgame, her children were using the time to begin their lives in earnest. Kathy met a fellow architect at Washington University by the name of Richard Bennett Lord. Luckily, he went by Bennett and not Richard, so there would be no confusion of names in the family. They married in 1973 on a Mississippi showboat, and Andre even attended, finding time between one or the other of his own weddings.

As for Barbara, returning to Rome had allowed her to reconnect with her old friend Marco Westerweel, who, along with his brother David Westerweel, had attended the Overseas School. David's family was Dutch and possessed a stately manor house in eastern Holland. The story of their wedding included an infamous tale of Andre at his best.

Being the "event father" that he was, Andre also chose to attend this wedding ceremony in Holland. He was staying at the Rotterdam Hilton, where his future son-in-law David worked the night shift on the desk. True to form, Andre asked his about-to-be son-in-law to arrange for a lady of the evening to come by the night before the wedding. Unfortunately, the evening escapade led to an untimely coronary "in the saddle." Andre was taken to the hospital where he was put into a double room with an Arab gentleman.

The wedding was postponed for a month, and it proved impossible to contain the story of cause and effect. Barbara took it in stride, but the Westerweel family certainly had an impression of Andre that they hadn't had before.

A truism about people who hustle is that they have to keep juggling or the balls hit the ground. With Andre in the hospital, his development hustles started to founder. Two days in, he called his son—Richard was a banker in New York City but then—and asked for help looking into the brokering of an oil tanker. This was so far afield from anything either Andre or Richard had experience with as to be ludicrous. Richard demurred.

Two weeks later, Andre passed through New York City on his way home and showed Richard the check he had received for $3 million for successfully brokering said oil tanker. The next day, Millie called Richard and told him that Andre had stiffed her for the $5,000 hospital telephone bill. She laughed it off as you might expect.

In the meantime, Richard had met Mary Jo Janak and proffered marriage. When she learned this, Millie was less than pleased. Her displeasure had nothing to do with Mary, whom she found delightful, but it reflected Millie's view that career should take precedence over love. This was perhaps the one time Richard openly disagreed with Millie and told her to mind her own business. Millie respected his view, but the appearance of his mother's gender bias in this instance—compared to her ready endorsement of his sister's marriage—made the issue troubling to Richard.

Unlike Millie, Andre had not learned his lesson. He decided that he would attend yet another wedding of one of his children. Richard was ambivalent about his father's attendance, but he found it more than a bit disingenuous when Andre gave him a set of gold sombrero cuff links. He would have made more of an impression if he had sent in the bike he had promised in 1963 or the car he had promised in 1971. But a set of gold sombrero cufflinks and one important piece of advice would have to do. Before going down the aisle, Andre told Richard to only let Italians cut his hair.

As she moved toward retirement, Millie was discovering a new side of Rome. She had been introduced to the Country Club of Rome. She had never before had time for such amusement. Now, with the kids gone and her program teams in place for the duration, she joined the club and took up her old favorite sport of golf. The club was out on the Via Apia Antica, and the drive out to the club was a pleasure she loved to share with all her visitors. The lush and regal-looking club was actually too expensive for Millie except that FAO professionals at the director level had received a special arrangement that put it within reach for her.

Millie at the Circolo de Golf di Roma

Millie decided to make full use of her last few years in Rome by inviting as many of her old friends as possible to come and visit her when they could. She took her work seriously and would have worked for years to come if FAO rules hadn't mandated retirement at the age of sixty-two. That rule had a strange effect on her, making her feel powerless to change the situation and causing her to get the most out of her time in Rome.

Millie at a fountain on the Janiculum Hill

CHAPTER 17

The Lady of Lagos
(Rome and Beyond, 1980–1981)

Millie enjoying "retirement" on the links

When Millie turned sixty-three, she graciously handed over the mantle of FAO authority to her successor, a woman from India. At first, she chose to stay in Rome and play some more golf—a fitting transition for a woman who had loved athletics as much as she had loved her work.

FAO had strict rules about limiting consulting arrangements with the agency after retirement, but Millie soon realized that there was a strong demand for her services—and she knew where there was a will there was a way. The trick was to find situations where FAO funding was not involved, but perhaps could be in the future if the project were properly reshaped. What was less clear in her mind was how much more of this sort of work she actually wanted to do. As already noted, there is a certain Sisyphean aspect to the work of regional development, whereby every inch of hillside over which one pushes the rock can be quickly and easily erased so that the work must start all over again.

Nevertheless, the only thing less rewarding to Millie than pushing that rock was *not* pushing it. Moreover, how much golf and relaxation can a spry youngster of sixty-four endure? Millie answered the call when one of Natalie Hahn's colleagues in Nigeria told her about a project that needed organizing and which, ironically, enjoyed funding from the Rockefeller Foundation. The project involved trying to stop desertification from spreading southward in the Republic of Niger from the northern border to the east of Niamey, the nation's capital. This undertaking would not be unlike what had been successfully done with the planting of orange trees in Israel's Judaea Desert. The idea was to plant fruit trees in the northeast sector of Nigeria as a natural brake on the encroaching desert. The trick was, as always in that part of the world, to find a way to tap into the aquifer sufficiently to give the fruit trees a chance to survive.

The north part of Nigeria is predominantly Muslim, and the Hausa-Fulani are the dominant tribal force. The good news was that the region was somewhat removed from the long-term civil war in the south between the Igbo and the Yoruba as well as from the corruption that accompanied the oil finds along the coast. The challenge would be to bring an entirely new agro-industry to a people accustomed to a nomadic existence. Millie had seen it all before and knew that the place to begin would be in Lagos— in the belly of the beast that was Nigeria.

Millie had been very successful in Venezuela in similar efforts with the Wayuu. Here, though, there was the overriding problem of national indebtedness that had been brought on by the government's purported attempts to build out a national infrastructure. With the world of finance awash in petrodollars, money had flowed freely into Nigeria and been syphoned away just as readily by the increasingly corrupt public and private machinery in Lagos. Millie's idea (or more accurately, Richard's idea, as a result of his newly found focus on the global debt crisis, which had erupted across the globe in 1982) was to take the bad sovereign debt the banks had incurred by lending too liberally to less developed countries (LDCs) like Nigeria and exchange it for productive equity investments in the country. This economic threat was further compounded by the encroaching Sahara to the north, which threatened to deepen and expand poverty throughout the country.

The market value of the Nigerian sovereign debt was declining daily. Indeed, the LDC debt problem was in full swing all around the world, as Eastern Europe, Africa, and even parts of Southeast Asia were experiencing the same trauma. If the strategy worked, Millie reckoned she might leave a path for her colleagues at FAO and other UN agencies—a path forward that would be both financially creative and developmentally constructive.

Capitalism is more or less a requirement for a successful equity holding. Africa was the logical venue to explore this newly conceived salvage technique, and nowhere in Western Africa was capitalism more entrenched systematically than in oil-rich Nigeria.

At this point, a minor digression on capitalism might be helpful. The country that borders Nigeria to the west is the oft-forgotten country of Benin, whose dubious claim to fame is that it served as the central transshipment point for much of the slave trade between Western Africa and the Southern United States. While the myth persists that Portuguese traders pillaged local tribes of natives for their strong young flesh, the truth is that local Benin chieftains, who were used to constant tribal warfare, cajoled Portuguese traders to get into the slave business since the chieftains figured they would have a limitless supply of captive warriors to sell them. So capitalism (linked with and fueled by cruelty and corruption) is inherent to West Africa.

Western banks already had a small presence in Africa, but most of their transactions were cross-border transactions. This meant that they had few people on the ground and even fewer strong contacts from which to base their explorations into interesting businesses to buy. Millie pondered this issue while she busied herself with planning out the fruit tree business model.

She began to receive letters, proposals, resumes, and telexes from all manner of Nigerian scavengers. She had barely set foot in country when news had spread that the she was working with a set of NGOs (nongovernmental organizations) to find debt-equity swap opportunities to fund her fruit tree project. Millie knew without even looking at these over-the-transom proposals that most would be from very unsavory and disreputable types. Consequently, she determined that the best way to proceed would be to find a few reputable local agents who might source interesting opportunities for her. She started to sift through the growing pile of letters and proposals to see if anything held promise.

One letter in particular caught her attention. It was from an Olumide Williams, and it was on Tiffany bond paper. The writer stated simply that he was very well connected in Nigeria, had been trained in the United States, and was available as a consultant for seeking out opportunities in Nigeria. He had enclosed his resume, which was impressive by any standards: Dartmouth undergraduate, Stanford MBA, a five-year internship with a large American multinational, and two years of experience working on countertrade transactions at a major American bank (basically barter deals). Millie contacted him immediately to arrange a meeting.

When she met Olumide Williams for breakfast at Rome's Hassler Roof hotel, Millie was very impressed by his seeming sophistication. Mide (as he asked everyone to call him) was tall, ebony dark, very handsome, and extremely poised. He was decked out for the occasion in the best that Brooks Brothers had to offer (specially tailored for sure) from collar bar to suspenders to spit-polished shoes. The meeting started with Millie posing the usual questions based on his resume. What sort of deals had he worked on? Had he done any debt-equity transactions? What kind of contacts did he have in Nigeria? Mide answered all of her questions politely and proficiently, and at the first lull, he launched into his pitch about what he had in mind for Millie's project. That he had been sent her proposal by a "local" in Nigeria seemed to validate his depth of contacts in the country, but at the same time, it worried Millie about his ethics.

Mide hinted that his family connections were very strong all across the country—extending beyond the current military regime—and also valid for working well with the governing clique. He showed excellent knowledge of the local economy and seemed to be familiar with most of the important companies and multinational subsidiaries in Nigeria. He also seemed to know exactly which buttons to push to get Millie's interest, inherently understanding what she would be willing to do and not do. He had her salivating over the funding deals he was certain he could quickly tee up. Interestingly, he also commanded the staff at the Hassler Roof as though they were his personal entourage, sending back his eggs Benedict because he felt the hollandaise sauce was too tart. Millie thought it was superb.

Needless to say, Millie immediately entered into contract negotiations with Mide. He seemed perfect. He preferred to work on a consulting basis. She arranged a contingency contract with a healthy percentage cut off the top of any deals done. Specifically, he wanted an asset-based fee that would scale up as the size of the deal increased. He impressed Millie with his shrewd negotiating skills. He even traded away his expense coverage in exchange for a higher percentage of deals done. Normally this would be ideal for Millie since it promised to keep her up-front costs to a minimum, but in this case, his supreme confidence made it seem unlikely to work in her favor in the long haul. Based on the amount of Nigerian debt that was potentially involved, Millie was certain that Mide would cash in big.

Mide immediately set about preparing for a trip to Nigeria to begin his explorations on her behalf. He included one visit to Rome in order to review his plans with Millie. On that visit, he introduced her to his fiancée, one of the most stunning young blonde American women Millie had ever seen. Her name was Rachel Feldman, and he introduced her as an attorney from New York. Millie found herself pondering the strangeness of it all and allowed herself to wonder whose father (Mide's or Rachel's) would be more upset at the news of their betrothal.

Mide left for Nigeria shortly thereafter, taking Rachel with him. Since this was to be the introductory visit for her with his family, Millie hoped that the fireworks wouldn't interfere with his mission. Soon Millie began receiving daily telexes from Mide containing all sorts of interesting ideas. It became a full-time job just to review his proposals.

By the time Mide came back to Rome, she had at least six interesting-sounding deals in the hopper. They were all what finance people call "two-cushion" shots (as in billiards), where one had to do one thing in order to get at another. There was a hotel-related deal in Lagos, an offshore oil deal involving a land swap, a mining opportunity where the phosphates being mined would be sold for fertilizer, and several other real estate trade situations. Mide seemed to have a nose for what would appeal to Millie and to be able to cut through Nigerian red tape and get to decision makers. She became more and more impressed. In the course of their meetings to review the work, Mide said that getting the deals off the ground would require Millie to make a trip with him to Lagos. She knew that it was the worst destination in the third world at the time and that several of her FAO predecessor had refused to go anywhere near Lagos. Her sense of adventure led her to agree, however, and she looked forward to coming home with a professionally organized public/private/ NGO deal of a new species. Little did she know what was in store for her in Lagos.

They organized the trip to coincide with a major African regional development meeting to be held in Abidjan, which was known as the Riviera of West Africa. She was joined on the trip by a colleague from the Rockefeller Foundation (one she had just met on this transaction) named Ted. After a few days at the Hilton and a round of golf and a swim at the Ivoire Country Club, Millie found herself beginning to like West Africa more than she had remembered from prior visits. Although she knew Lagos would not be as nice, the preliminaries were putting her in a fine mood. The trek to Lagos was to be done via Air Afrique. The flight was billed as a lunch flight, but they were unclear how this would take place since there was no flight attendant. This was clarified in flight when the captain announced that they would be landing in Togo for lunch. As they were disembarking amid a thong of locals, Millie looked at the ramshackle terminal building where their lunch was presumably waiting and reflected to Ted with amazement that Togo had one vote in the UN just as the United States did.

When their party arrived in Lagos, they were greeted by a smiling man holding a sign with the project's fruit tree logo on it. They went to him, and he insisted on taking their hand luggage even though he was at least a full head shorter than either Millie or Ted. Ted had been to Lagos before and had met this fellow, whom he described as by far the best local "expediter" or "fixer," a seemingly common job description in Nigeria. His job was to smooth out all the red tape and whatever else needed smoothing so that they could get out of the airport and be on their way. He did his job flawlessly, walking them right through immigration and doing much the same for them with their bags in the customs area. Judging by the lines of tired-looking people in the airport, it might have taken them hours to get out of the airport on their own.

A black Chrysler sedan was waiting for them outside the terminal. The expediter waved good-bye to them as their hired driver sped off toward the city. After asking the driver how long it would take to get to town and realizing that she only understood about half of his answer in pidgin English, Millie chose to forego conversation and watch the scenery go by.

It was quite a show to observe, with people walking along both sides of the road in hordes. Although it was unclear where they were going, they all kept moving. Every few hundred feet, there seemed to be someone sleeping on the side of the road. Then, as they passed a light post with a body hanging from it, they realized that the prone bodies were not sleeping at all. Millie now remembered that she had heard about this road in a story about a trip Henry Kissinger had made to Lagos. On that occasion, the advance Secret Service squad, in cooperation with the advance State Department squad, had supposedly prepared for the secretary of state's visit by having the road cleared several hours before his arrival at the airport. Despite these preparations, there were reportedly five dead bodies along the road as Kissinger drove into town. When Kissinger asked why these bodies had not been cleared that morning, the Secret Service assured him that they had. It seemed that five new bodies appearing in the space of two hours was par for the course along this road.

Millie had been told that the party would not be staying in a hotel since Lagos was one of the few cities in the world where there were no safe hotels for foreigners. There had been a Holiday Inn, but its security system had been overrun by prostitutes and thieves so that it was unsafe even in the confines of one's room. Although Holiday Inn had abandoned the operation of the property, it had not as yet been successful in retrieving its sign since the squatters felt it added a touch of class to the premises. Instead of a hotel, Mide had arranged for them to borrow a compound from an English insurance company with extensive interests in Nigeria. The compound was currently vacant as they searched feverishly for someone in their ranks willing to take a tour of duty in Lagos. If one could be found, he or she would get a double promotion and an enormous combat pay stipend. In addition, the compound would come equipped with nine servants, including cook and driver. There would also be eight R & R trips out of Lagos per year paid for by the company. Despite all of these inducements, the Lagos post was still vacant, allowing Millie and Ted to spend the next two nights there.

The first thing that struck a visitor about Lagos was that all the roads seem to be bounded by concrete ditches. Such ditches even graced the relatively upscale suburban community of Victoria, which had been the home of the wealthiest of the colonials when the Union Jack had flown over Nigeria. In Victoria, there were large, stately homes all around, all gradually succumbing to the humid African seaside climate. There were old men sitting, hunched up in front of nearly every gate, serving as "guards" though they looked as if they could do little more than yell for help. The entourage pulled to a stop in front of one such gate with its attendant guard. As they waited for it to open, Millie glanced into the ditch and was disgusted to see that it was an open sewer in which human refuse floated. Even though the window was closed, she could imagine the stench.

After a very restless night spent listening to the fifteen-year-old window air conditioner struggle against the formidable heat and humidity, Millie awoke to the trials of communicating with the houseboy about breakfast. She hadn't seen Mide since they arrived, but he was scheduled to join her any minute. The iron gates of the compound opened, and a dark Mercedes limousine drove in. As it pulled up to the front, she noticed that the rear door had something sticking out of it. The door opened, and there was Mide in all his glory. His six-foot-three frame was adorned with a long flowing robe of white with gold threading. His close-cropped hair was covered by a matching Nigerian pillbox-style hat. She knew it was Mide because he immediately started to curse in his best prep school English when he realized that he had caught his beautiful robe in the door of the car—and it had dragged through the streets of Lagos on the way to see Millie.

Mide paused to deliver his greetings and went in search of the houseboy in a futile attempt to clean the hem of his robe. When he rejoined the team, he apologized for the faux pas and began to go over the plans for the day. They would meet with a series of influential Nigerian businessmen who would either be key to getting the approvals they needed to do the desired transactions or the owners of properties they wanted to include in the debt-swap transaction. He suggested that they be on their way.

As they rode through the streets of Lagos, Millie asked Mide if he wore his national dress often. Since his garb looked very new, she wondered if he had had it made specially for the occasion. He said that he often wore similar national dress at cocktail receptions, on national holidays, and for any number of serious business meetings where national issues were involved. Millie joked that he didn't seem to have much experience wearing it in cars since he almost caught it in the door again when they left the compound.

Their first stop was to meet the governor at the Central Bank, where they were told to go to the fifth floor. When the elevator stopped instead on the sixth, they asked the attendant why it hadn't gone to five. He politely explained that the elevator was broken and would not stop there. They walked down one flight and eventually found the governor's office. He kept them waiting for half an hour. It surprised her when the governor did not seem to really know Mide. When the latter introduced himself, she did notice the governor nodding his head when he mentioned his father's name. It was a cordial but very unproductive meeting. The governor explained that he was not altogether certain that debt-equity swaps would be in Nigeria's best interests. He pretended not to understand their arguments to the contrary. They left feeling somewhat confused until Mide explained that the governor was a political crony of the military head of state who knew little about economics but whose approval could be easily secured for any deal Mide and Millie wanted. Millie's unease was growing as she listened to this story.

The next meeting with a powerful local businessman was totally different. Uniformed guards at the gate snapped to attention when they saw the limo. As the visitors got out of the car, their host began with a hug for Mide and firm handshakes for Ted and Millie. The businessman reminded Millie of Dick Gregory in his expensive-looking slacks and loose-fitting open-collared shirt. From the beautiful cobblestone courtyard with a fountain, they were taken into a marvelous home with an extensive collection of native African artifacts mixed in casually with the very best of Western furniture. There was an original Eames chair in one corner and what looked like a Napoleonic desk and chair in another. They were offered coffee and native sweet cakes. The meeting went like clockwork, and their host spent most of the time telling them how easy it would be to get approval to do what they wanted. He could help with the approvals, and there were no shortages of good, reasonably priced properties for sale. He would gladly assist them even if it was not one of his properties. He said he believed in his country and wanted to do all he could to promote its growth. He carried on about Mide and how proud he and his friends were of him and his success in the United States.

Before leaving, Millie asked to use the restroom and was directed to one, equally lavish and modern, by the foyer. She noted that the copy of the *New Yorker* on a small shelf was only four days old. As she was exiting from the restroom, she noticed a young black woman with a Walkman on her ears bouncing down the stairs, wearing cutoff jeans and a T-shirt with UCLA emblazoned across the front. At the bottom of the stairs, she stopped and saw Mide. Before looking into the living room, she burst out with a great big, "Hi, Mide! What in the world are you doing in that getup?"

Although Mide didn't see Millie watching, he shushed the girl, pressing up against her with an index finger on her lip. Millie imagined he was saying, "Don't blow my cover. I'm working the crowd." With that, Millie made her entry into the foyer whereupon Mide introduced her to their host's daughter. They said their good-byes to everyone and went on their way without any mention of the incident. Mide asked in the limo if Millie had found that to be a more agreeable meeting. She nodded but thought to herself that Brooks Brothers had no place in Africa.

Millie and Ted were both relieved to get out of Lagos. Mide continued to send them proposals and telexes for months, but they never paid him a dime for them. Nor did they ever transact a swap deal in Africa. The last Millie heard of Mide, he was back in the United States living in New Canaan, Connecticut, with Rachel and her children. He had bought a chain of car washes and was busy turning them into upscale auto-detailing centers. Meanwhile, Nigerian debt was continuing to trade at twelve cents on the dollar—and there were still no safe hotels in Lagos.

Millie among the fruit trees in Nigeria

Millie did spend six months in the field in northeastern Nigeria, working on a straight grant proposal for the fruit trees rather than a fancy financially engineered deal like a debt swap. While the area was pretty basic, it was far less dangerous and corrupt than Lagos.

She enjoyed her month in Nigeria and made friends with many locals as well as expats who were working toward the same goals of stemming desertification. As always, Millie made the best of her surroundings, going so far as to play several rounds of golf at a makeshift club built by some Australian aid workers. The most notable aspect of the play was that instead of putting on the green, one putted on the "brown" since the putting surface was sand oiled down to be hard and smooth. Millie actually found the course fun, and using dirt piles for tees was a throwback to the old days of golf that she enjoyed.

Millie left the region with a fully prepared and packaged fruit tree plan worthy of funding. Unfortunately, it was unlikely to see the light of day in a country whose priorities went more to the needs of the ruling elite than the rural poor and starving.

CHAPTER 18

Video Poker Grandma
(Las Vegas, Nevada, 1981–1991)

Millie surrounded by four of her seven grandkids

After her experience in Nigeria, Millie was contemplating packing up to leave Rome when she was contacted by an old Brazilian friend who had a project in the south near the city of Porto Alegre in the province of Rio Grande do Sul. Porto Alegre is just north of Uruguay, the most capitalistic of Latin American countries, and just east of Paraguay, at the time the longest-running dictatorship in Latin America and a "closed" state run by

General Alfredo Stroessner. Needing a funding proposal written, Millie's friend invited her to come and enjoy the pleasures that Brazil had to offer, while helping her by putting the extensive development proposal together. Millie had not spent much time in Brazil since it was a relatively progressive country. While it certainly had pockets of severe poverty, it was generally much more advanced than most developing countries. The prospect of a long visit intrigued Millie, and she accepted her friend's offer.

In some ways, Porto Alegre was the perfect final development assignment for her. Most importantly, it was in Latin America. Her Spanish served her well since that area of Brazil spoke more Spanish than Portuguese. It was tropical, but not too junglelike in its lushness—in that respect, a positive change from the dry climate of northern Nigeria—and her beloved fruit trees grew like weeds. The most interesting aspect of her experience there was that she managed to find living quarters in an old convent. She took her simple meals in silence with the nuns and lived a Spartan existence in a plain, bare room with a crucifix over the single, hard bed. Other than her bed, the room contained only a writing desk and a chair. In the convent, one worked by day and slept or prayed by night. Millie was not religious, but she was spiritual. The extended time for contemplation and self-focus seemed perfect to her at that moment in her life.

In that peaceful, simple setting, Millie was able to put her life's work into context. She was able to think about all she had done and the people about whom she cared most. This contemplative time had a cleansing and purifying impact on her that was unlike anything she had ever experienced. She finished the complicated proposal in several months, to the great satisfaction of her friend who had commissioned it. She felt centered and right with her world, making the decision that it was time for her to permanently leave Rome.

Since FAO gave its employees only one expatriation move to their home country, Millie had to pick the place to which she would retire. Having spent her life on the move, this was not a clear-cut decision. Her children were scattered widely across the United States. Richard lived in New York City, working with reasonable success on Wall Street. Kathy was an architect living in Mazomanie, Wisconsin, an area familiar to Millie. Barbara lived in Las Vegas, where she and her husband had emigrated from Holland under a Dutch program to encourage depopulation of the small country. Millie wasn't sure what she wanted in retirement, but she knew that neither New York nor Mazomanie would do. Las Vegas, on the other hand, was warm and moderately priced, and it was a place through which nearly everyone seemed to pass or could at least visit without much trouble. The more she considered it, the more it seemed the perfect retirement community for her. After thirteen years of humid Roman weather, warm and dry was the right formula.

Before heading to Las Vegas, Millie stopped into Mazomanie for a visit with Kathy, Bennett, and their son, Alex. If her new life would involve learning how to be a grandmother, she might as well practice on the oldest: five-year-old Alex. Kathy was also due to give birth to her daughter, Stephanie, but while Millie wanted to be helpful, it was clear that Kathy and Bennett had their affairs under control. In any case, after a few weeks in Wisconsin, Millie remembered why she had chosen Las Vegas as the place to ship her belongings.

In Las Vegas, Millie chose an apartment in Las Vegas Towers on Flamingo Boulevard in the eastern part of town. The complex was near Barbara's home and had a swimming pool, of which both she and Barbara's family would make full use. It had the added attraction of being near the University of Nevada Las Vegas, which had all the advantages common to a large public university.

Barb and Dave lived in a small garden apartment that was just sufficient for them and their son Jason, who was just a few months younger than his cousin Alex. Millie's daughters seemed to be on a choreographed cycle; Barbara was also again pregnant. Since Dave and Barb both worked to make ends meet, Millie immediately pitched in to help the young family with childcare, housekeeping, and general moral support.

When it came time for Barbara to deliver, Dave and Millie took her to the birthing clinic, which helped her have her daughter and return home on the same day. It may have been Barbara's plan even before Millie showed up, but it was clearly more feasible with her help. The episode was also entirely consistent with Millie's worldview since she viewed birth and death as natural acts requiring only minimal attention. She may have worked for forty years to help women improve their lot and escape the need to have their children in the fields so as not to miss work, but she completely respected the ethos that such workaday birthing represented.

She was proud that her daughter was doing the modern equivalent. Millie and Barbara happily brought home their new baby girl, Nichole.

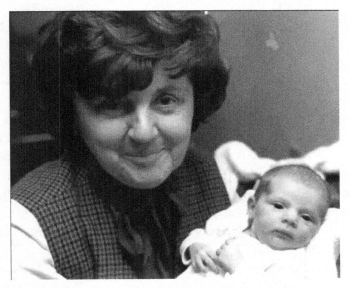

Millie with newborn Nichole

Meanwhile, in New York, Richard and Mary were awaiting their first child. Richard was rising rapidly through the ranks in banking, while Mary was preparing to retire as a small company office manager in order to be a full-time mother. Whereas Kathy and Barbara were following their mother's path of combining motherhood and work, Mary was following her own mother's role model by focusing on full-time motherhood. Richard and Mary's son Roger was born in mid-1982, putting Millie into the grandmother role on all three fronts.

At almost the same time, Andre—who had invested his $3 million oil-tanker windfall in an altogether new life—married for the sixth (or so) time to a woman named Bobbi. He had started a development business in Visalia, a town in California's San Joaquin Valley. Visalia was in the midst of a transformation from a purely agricultural area dependent on migrant farm workers into a more vertically integrated food-producing area. Food-processing plants were making it possible for workers to find year-round employment in the area, thereby eliminating the migrant aspect of their existence. Suddenly, many workers were in need of housing, and Andre was eager to cash in by meeting this need. In this undertaking, he partnered with an elderly Polish farmer with lots of land, little interest in continuing to farm, and susceptibility to a fast-talker like Andre.

Andre formed Marin Enterprises, putting his name on the top of the tallest building in Visalia (perhaps six stories high). His initial planning was for a development of four hundred inexpensive homes in a pancake-flat portion of the valley. He already had the requisite antebellum mansion with the iron gates and the backyard apiary, and he already breakfasted daily with the local men of influence. To move this project to the next level, however, he needed a captive architecture firm. Despite the University of Padua diploma on his office wall, he knew he needed a professional. He wasted no time offering Kathy and Bennett a proverbial deal they couldn't refuse. While being able to start their own firm was great incentive, their acceptance of the deal proffered by Andre was all about healing Kathy's wounds of youth and allowing her to get closer to her father at long last.

While Millie was settling into Vegas Towers, Kathy, Bennett, Alex, and Stephanie began their own resettlement into the real Middle America of Visalia. Andre had also asked Richard to consider moving to Visalia to found and operate a chartered national bank for him. While Richard was still impressed by his father's oil tanker deal, he was neither a small-town banker nor did he buy into the idea of vertical integration between a real estate developer and a bank. Unlike architecture and development, banking was intentionally an arm's length business that could run into serious trouble if a too-chummy relationship grew up between the bank and its client.

Richard's instinct to steer clear was well placed. Ethical foundation is a slippery slope. The man ultimately hired by Andre to set up the bank was, indeed, a bad actor who embezzled money with Andre's countersignature. This unfortunate occurrence unfolded at the same time that Andre was becoming successful enough with the development company that he had started to take generous allowances for himself. He bought a private plane, started taking long foreign vacations, and generally began to loosen the reins. Before he knew it, Andre was crosswise with the law and was indicted for fraud.

This series of missteps caused Andre's legitimate development empire to collapse almost immediately. In the manner of hustlers dropping balls when they go on the lam, he didn't imperil only vendors and partners; this time, he was bankrupting his own daughter and her family. These calamitous developments made Millie sick with concern. Kathy and Bennett left Visalia literally in the dead of night and resolved not to communicate with Andre ever again. Richard felt the breeze of the missed bullet that figuratively parted his hair. Andre soon turned himself in and was acquitted as the innocent dupe of a sleazy banker's ploy. That outcome changed nothing for Kathy, who would forever remember that her father had put her well-being low on his list of priorities—a hard realization for any child and particularly devastating for Kathy.

As the eighties unfolded and Kathy and Bennett struggled to get back on their feet, Richard was tasked by his bank to recover $4 billion in Latin American debt during the global debt crisis. When Millie, who was happily helping Barbara raise her family and entertaining visiting friends in Las Vegas, learned about Richard's new posting, she had a bit to say: "So I spent forty years putting money into Latin America, and you're now making a career out of taking money out of Latin America?" Richard was able to roll out his sanctity-of-contracts arguments, but especially in the face of Millie's withering criticisms, it was hard to feel good about the situation, regardless of his belief that what he was doing was important, worthwhile, and righteous. The whole episode motivated him to start working with CARE, the global relief and development giant.

CARE became a passion of Richard's for thirty years, ultimately culminating in a nine-year term on its board of directors. He traveled with CARE to places like India, Benin, and Guatemala, getting so involved after several trips to Guatemala that he gave hundreds of thousands of dollars to CARE to build out girls' education programs in Central America. He did this specifically to honor Millie. In a very direct way, his commitment to CARE had grown out of his belief in her life's work, a sense of guilt about his emerging markets work, and his undying respect for his mother.

Millie with Richard, Roger, and Carolyn

By this time, Millie's extended brood consisted of her own three children, each with two offspring of their own (Richard and Mary had produced their second child, Carolyn, in 1986). The grandchildren were symmetrical sets of boy/girl in each family. The whole clan gathered together regularly at Richard's Utah vacation home to ski in winter and golf and cavort in the summer. Fittingly, the ever-athletic Millie was now matriarch of a squad of like-minded kids and grandkids.

In 1993, one such family ski trip was interrupted by a call notifying the family that Andre (an incurable lifelong smoker) had died of a heart attack at the age of seventy in the driveway of his modest home in Carlsbad, California. Strangely enough, he had been living in the same county as Kathy and Bennett but never knew it since Bennett and Kathy held to their resolve never to have further contact with him.

The family members all flew from Utah to San Diego to say good-bye to Andre and to deal with the family matters attendant to his death. The way Richard saw it, this event allowed him to become a man at the age of thirty-nine. The critical moment came when he was standing in the courtyard of the Mission San Luis Rey overlooking the hazy Southern California coast. In his hand was a machined brass box, in his pocket was a plastic Ziploc bag, and in his heart was a combined sense of humor and forgiveness.

He was there to bury Andre. Before him in this shaded and flowered spot stood Millie, Kathy, Barbara, Shirley, Bobbi, Diane, Sondra, and a number of other people unknown to him. Richard suspected that some of them were creditors, some were ex-lovers, and some may even have been other wives and half-siblings, for all he knew. Andre had lived a full life. As his eldest son, it had fallen to Richard to handle all the arrangements for his father. All was now complete except for the eulogy, which he was about to deliver.

This would be Richard's last opportunity to make a statement about this man who had charmed and disappointed him and so many others. This Freudian moment was among Richard's finest hours. He told it like it was. There was humor in his choice of euphemism as he described the man as being complex in all his ways. When Richard mentioned that even his father's business dealings were complex, there was an audible chuckle from the crowd—all of whom knew that Andre had been one of the most charming hustlers they had ever met. The defining sentence of the eulogy was an acceptance of all these peccadilloes, an acknowledgement of the man's good qualities, and the forgiveness of a father by his son for all the promises not kept.

As the crowd drifted away with nary a dry eye, Richard turned to deal with placing the brass box containing Andre's ashes into the small crypt in the mission wall. The crypt had been made for two boxes, and Andre's current wife Bobbi had asked to be placed next to him for the hereafter. The ensuing discussion of whether to have the plate include her name or not was a memorable debate between the merits of uniform patina versus the premature acceptance of death.

The mission's funeral director was a compassionate soul who insisted on embracing all her charges and mashing her ample bosom to their chests for extended periods of time. Andre would certainly have appreciated Rosa's genuine and sensual expression of sorrow. After handing Richard the brass box, she gave him the Ziploc bag containing the extra ashes of his father that would not fit in the box. When Richard asked Rosa what he should do with them, she shrugged and gave him another hug. He felt better for no particular reason.

As Richard pushed the box into the crypt and looked at the extra room left for Bobbi's box, the solution to the problem became self-evident. The Ziploc bag would join the rest of its remains until such time as someone would open the crypt to introduce Bobbi's box therein. By then, nature would probably have resolved the issue, but if Ziploc were to live up to its advertised staying power, it would simply become someone else's problem. Richard had fulfilled his obligations. He had taken care of business. He had paid all the bills (certainly more than Andre had ever done for Richard), and he had sent all Andre's mourners away with tears in their eyes.

To the end, Andre was hard to define. He held unusual power over all the members of his family, especially—and always—Millie. He was certainly too big to box, either physically or psychologically. But in his passing, he did give Richard the opportunity to become a man.

Andre left all his daughters and his other son (from a México City marriage that was annulled after it was learned that he had previously been married to Millie in the same church) with massive holes in their hearts and minds. Richard wished all his siblings had possessed his ability to achieve closure as he had done somewhere between the Neptune Society and the Mission San Luis Rey. For her part, Millie adjusted smoothly as she had always done, finding it easy to socialize with all of Andre's ex-wives and other children. She had long since found her peace with Andre.

Millie leaning on her townhouse in Las Vegas

CHAPTER 19

The Cowboy Lullaby
(Las Vegas, Nevada, 1991–2017)

Millie and Irving at their sixtieth Cornell reunion

Millie had never been a big reunion buff. Some people (especially at Cornell) set their personal clocks by their reunion cycle. She had indulged herself by going to her fiftieth reunion in 1987, but that was as much to visit with Aggie and the rest of her Ithaca family as to reconnect with former classmates.

While in Ithaca for that event, she stopped by to see her old friend Lawrence Kohler, whose wife Louise had been one of Millie's college pals.

Louise had passed away, and Lawrence—a successful precision machine shop owner in Ithaca—was a sportsman and hunter/fisherman of the ultimate order. Millie and Lawrence had been good friends over the years in a passing way, but he particularly remembered Millie as the sportswoman she had been. The three of them had made many trips together to ski Tuckerman's Ravine. He and Louise (or Weezy, as she was known) had also become nationally ranked clay pigeon shooters. Lawrence was lonely and happy to see his old friend. Millie recognized the twinkle in his eye and was not surprised when he called her a few weeks later and told her he wanted to come out to Las Vegas to see her.

Millie was wary of Lawrence since she knew that Louise and he had had a particularly tempestuous relationship over the years. Lawrence was a man's man, and as much as he liked his women sporting, he was set in his ways and wanted a female companion simply to sign on to his life program as it was, including maintaining a home base in Ithaca and prolonged absences while he fished and hunted the Yukon. Millie was flattered by his attention, but she declined with great care so as not to damage a wonderful fifty-year friendship and more good memories than she could count.

As the fifty-fifth reunion approached in 1992, she received a surprising call from a classmate who had not even shown up for the fiftieth. The call was from none other than Irving Jenkins, her charming friend of crew team and Golden Gloves memory and the undergraduate-era fiancé of her old friend Kay Hughes. No one at the last reunion had heard of or from Irving in years. Kay, who was married to her second husband (a radical economics professor at Cornell) and living in Ithaca, had not heard a peep from him since 1937.

After his summer in Hawaii in 1937 and his decision to stay on to run the Del Monte pineapple plantation on the Big Island, he had married and had a son, Irving Jr. Following many years of enjoying regular horseback riding and island living, Irving and his wife had moved at first to the Northwestern United States and eventually settled down in Delray Beach, Florida. Their son stayed on and became an artist in Hawaii. In Florida, his wife had contracted cancer, and Irving had spent several years caring lovingly for her until she passed on. Millie was touched by his story, which had a sweet, but melancholy air about it. This six-foot-four, 240-pound man had become a bit of a gentle giant with a serious dose of Eastern philosophy and Zen-like ways.

Like Lawrence, Irving was lonely as a widower. He started courting Millie with great zeal. It was wonderful for her to be reminded of all the great times in Ithaca when she and Kay and Irving and Weezy and Lawrence had hung around together. Irving was very sweet. He wore his cowboy hat and Clark Gable mustache with great panache. He had a deep voice that rumbled from his throat very slowly and with great purpose. He laughed easily. A notable character trait was that whenever Irving was asked how he was, instead of saying, "Fine, thanks," he would always say, "Better and better!" with great gusto. In some ways, this was Irving's defining philosophy. Nothing in the past or present mattered—just the future, which was always rosier than the present moment. Irving always made everyone around him feel good. He certainly made Millie feel good.

Irving said that Millie should move to Delray Beach with him. Millie liked Irving, but she was unmoved. Her comment to her children at the time was that he was a nice man for whom she cared deeply, but that she had no intentions of upending her life and moving to tropical Florida. "No more tropics for me!"

Irving did what a man on a mission would do; he changed tack. He declared that he was moving to Las Vegas.

Virtually all of Millie's contemporaries with whom she was still in contact knew and liked Irving a great deal. Unfortunately, Kay had recently passed away, but Aggie, Art, Lawrence, and brother Paul all remembered Irving fondly.

Millie, Irving, and Millie's brother Paul

177

Irving followed through on his promise, buying a townhouse condo in Las Vegas in a pleasant, but modest gated community. He asked Millie for help in making the selection, treading ever so lightly on the delicate balance that this was to be his place, but one that she might like as well, for who knows what reason. He sold his Delray Beach condo and committed himself to Las Vegas and the pursuit of his dreams.

It did not take long for Millie to decide that it was only economical and rational to take up Irving's offer to have her move in with him. She was spending a great deal of time there anyway. Wisely, he had decorated only minimally so there was room for any and all of Millie's things. By that stage of her life, Millie had become an experienced mover and an old hand at triaging belongings. Millie and Irving had clearly become an official "item," doing everything together. They traveled to see each other's old friends and haunts together. They went together to visit places on their respective bucket lists that needed seeing. All the while, Irving held open a formal and stated proposal of marriage. Millie, however, saw no point in that. She was an enlightened adult who felt no need for a marriage certificate.

The best reward for a job well done in the Marin/Jenkins family was to receive a foot rub from Irving. He had learned his reflexology technique in Hawaii and applied it generously and often to all members of the family. It came in particularly handy during the many foreign trips that he and Millie took together. Millie was starting to like this arrangement and this gentle but strong man.

Finally, in 1993 at the age of seventy-six, Millie declared that she and Irving had gone to Clark County Hall, obtained a marriage license, and gotten married. She treated the news as a foregone conclusion, inevitable and of little import. To her surprised children, she offered the explanation that it had been important to Irving, that she loved him a great deal, and that she had wanted to make him happy. The implicit message was that, though the institution of marriage meant little to her, the love of such a fine man meant a great deal.

Millie and Irving became inseparable. When they traveled anywhere, they always sat together and held hands. Clearly a strong bond had formed, filled with great affection. Although older people can often become less patient with each other's quirks and foibles, Millie and Irving were always fun loving and fully accepting of each other's eccentricities. They laughed together every day as they read each other the *Wall Street Journal* (a phenomenon that amazed Richard as a finance professional since neither had ever shown an interest in financial life as far as he knew, and he found little or no humor in the *Journal*). Both Millie and Irving had led amazingly accomplished and full lives and now seemed delighted to blend them into one and to dabble in small investments as much for fun as for profit.

The shared heritage of Cornell was also a great bond for the two. They had common and wonderful memories of their years there in the thirties and often spoke of the way they were. Whenever they traveled to Ithaca (perhaps twice a year), they stayed with Aggie and Art, who were of their vintage and shared many of the same memories.

During this time, family demographics had changed a bit. Richard had amicably separated from Mary and had remarried. He and Carol added another boy to the brood of grandkids, naming him Thomas. With the addition of Thomas, Millie now had seven grandchildren with a nineteen-year age spread. Although Millie was concerned about the tumult that divorce and remarriage may have caused in Richard's life, she was strongly supportive of him and his life decisions. She recognized some of his father's traits in her son, regardless of whether Richard himself embraced or eschewed those traits. Millie's father's coin collection and cigar box had been passed on to Richard, who had split it into two: a collection of the most valuable coins in their original 1964 sleeves and a smaller, formal grouping framed for display of the most visually interesting coins. Richard passed the former collection on to his eldest son Roger (sitting in his mother's safe-deposit box) and held the other "show" coins for Thomas. His hope was that this diversification of important family heirlooms would ensure the passing down through the family the Uher family values he so much admired.

Over the years, Richard had become increasingly engaged with Cornell. He had warm memories from his five years on campus, during which he earned a BA in economics and government in 1975 and an MBA in finance the following year. But more than feeling of simple nostalgia and affection for his alma mater, he felt a bond with the university because it was a shared connection between himself and Millie and her roots in

Myers. The family connection in Ithaca had even been strengthened by having worked flipping burgers one summer for his uncle Paul at the old roadhouse on Route 34B, the Corner Cupboard Restaurant.

This strong sense of connection explains why, soon after attending his twentieth business school reunion in 1996, Richard made the decision to look for a second home in Ithaca. Since he had fonder memories of the Cornell golf course than anywhere else in town, when he noticed a For Sale sign on an old ramshackle farmhouse near the course on Warren Road, he acted immediately.

The house was actually on offer by the university for a ninety-nine-year leasehold. From his experience in banking, Richard was familiar enough with the leasehold concept not to be too put off; he contracted almost on the spot to take over the place and renovate it to his liking. By chance, Millie and Irving were in town for a visit at the time. Richard asked them to come take a look. The ever-realistic Millie walked around the decrepit old house with its tilting floors and student-painted day-glow paint on the walls and calmly said, "I spent years trying to get away from old upstate farmhouses like this—and here you are buying into one. Do you have a clue what you are doing?" It was not the reaction for which Richard had hoped, but he was undeterred.

The gauntlet thrown, Richard said that he would be inviting the entire class of 1937 to his new house for a barbecue for their sixtieth reunion the following June—a mere nine months away. He audaciously boasted that Millie and Irving would not recognize the place by then.

Richard set about his task, managing the renovation from afar with the help of the relatively underemployed local contracting market. He was lucky that Ithaca had a mild winter that year, allowing the much-more-extensive-than-expected renovations to be completed. Although it would undoubtedly have been cheaper to tear down and rebuild than to renovate, the result was a beautiful upstate New York Colonial with a wraparound porch, a carriage house, a lovely (if highly seasonal) pool, and a garden that mimicked the surrounding Robert Trent Jones golf course with its attendant Ithaca stone walls.

Richard even found a stone and metal life-sized sculpture of Socrates that he placed on a stone pedestal in the backyard. The statue had sat in front of the Gutman Library at Harvard for years, but it had never been officially purchased by that university. When Richard bought it from the eighty-three year-old sculptor, he derived great enjoyment from the vision of Harvard's reeling from the loss of *its* Socrates to upstart Cornell. In the meantime, the harried workmen at the site amused themselves by placing sneakers on Socrates's feet and a beer can in his outstretched hand.

At eleven o'clock on the morning of the sixtieth-reunion barbecue, Richard evicted the last of the painters from the site and proudly welcomed the class of 1937 to his new Ithaca home. It was a very special day to honor Millie's and Irving's Cornell legacy and the rampant and occasionally unbounded enthusiasm for achievement that Richard had inherited from Millie.

Millie and Irving at Buckingham Palace Mall

Irving and Millie spent their final years together traveling the world. Irving showed Millie his beloved Hawaii, and Millie showed him her beloved Rome. They also traveled together to Israel and Mexico, and on the occasion of her eightieth birthday celebration, they accompanied Richard and his family to England on the final voyage of the HMS *Queen Elizabeth II*. Final voyages may be symbolic adventures, but there was definitely nothing final about that trip for Irving and Millie.

The fun-loving couple made full use of the Las Vegas casinos. They especially loved all the free casino swag, which they would save up over the year and then put in a big wrapped box like a piñata for their grandkids.

The grandchildren would open the boxes and not stop laughing until the last stupid giveaway came out of the newspaper wrappings. Millie and Irving also enjoyed the bargain buffets, with Irving always good for several plate-loads. Both of them became so enamored with video poker that Barbara finally bought them a used video poker machine so that they could play in their living room. In the later stages of their life together, they often exchanged disapproving comments about the low payouts from the machine, disregarding the fact that nothing was being put in on the front end.

On Millie's ninetieth birthday, the entire clan, including all seven grandchildren, gathered in Las Vegas for a tribute to her and Irving, who was several years older. A rousing "Happy Birthday" was sung by the throng around a large cake with a fearsome array of candles on top, after which several wrapped casino swag gifts for the matriarch drew hearty laughter.

Millie and her "cowboy" Irving

Irving died a peaceful death in 2009 at the age of ninety-five while sitting in a lounge chair in the living room of the couple's condo. As a large man his whole life, he had naturally and eventually encountered congestive heart failure as his heart worked harder and harder to keep up with him. Irving had been fond of saying, "Big dogs lead shorter, but more interesting lives." He was one big dog that never sat on the porch, instead always out joyously mixing it up with the world.

Millie, Nichole, and great-granddaughter Kaitlin

Without her sidekick, Millie went on a sort of autopilot. Her toughened body, which had been tested in the forge of the emerging markets of the world, was immune to practically everything. She was one tough bird. When she finally decided that enough was enough, she had reached the ripe age of one hundred and had three great-grandchildren. Kathy, Barb, and Richard were all with her for her final lap. Fittingly, Barbara, her primary caregiver for many years was alone with her when she passed on February 6, 2017—having waited to let her granddaughter Nichole (the one she had helped birth) say farewell. She spent her final fourteen days in the hospital and hospice refusing food or water in a final gesture that seemed to say that there were others in the world who needed it more than she. The dignity of her passing was quiet but profound.

Today Show hundred-year tribute to Millie

One thing that Richard and Millie shared was a desire to support Cornell in every way possible. The university had done well by both of them (as well as Irving), and it would later be the alma mater for five of Millie's seven grandchildren and who knows how many of her great grandchildren. In tribute, Richard established a series of scholarships in Millie's and Irving's names and donated to a number of causes at both the business school and the arts and sciences school, including a large atrium reading room named in their joint honor. In recognition of these gifts, Millie and Richard were both placed in the ranks of Foremost Benefactors and Builders of the university, and their names were etched in stone on the McGraw Terrace. This meant a great deal to both of them since only a very select group of alumni in the 150 years of Cornell have been so honored. The honor was enhanced for mother and son because it meant that they would be next to each other on that stone wall for eternity, overlooking Ithaca and the Cornell campus.

Millie and Richard at Cornell's "Builder's Wall"

Millie may have qualified as an icon for all she did in her life. She gave back to the world far more than she took. All she ever wanted in payment was what her father John always wanted: just a cold beer, thanks.

Millie enjoying her signature drink

EPILOGUE

John Uher was a man of action when he needed to be. He got him and his younger brother out of a bad place in Slovakia. He provided for his family in whatever way was necessary. He gave his family the better life that all parents wish for their children. John did not live to see Millie achieve her greatest successes. It's fair to suggest that he died worried that she was alone and with limited means for her children.

Oddly, Millie never worried about money for herself or her children. The best evidence was that rather than cashing in her father's rare coin collection to feed her brood, she treasured it as a symbol of her father's bootstrapped life and priorities. Tradition and achievement mattered, but money itself did not. She muddled through and taught her children to do likewise.

Millie lived life to the max. At every stage of her life, she was always looking forward and pushing herself to achieve. She was less idealist and fully a pragmatist, but she believed in the importance of helping others. She admired Margaret Mead for her groundbreaking research with indigenous tribes, but where Mead left off, Millie picked up to observe their lives and change them for the better.

Her roots and the times she lived through implied a likely propensity for a conservative take on the world, but she chose otherwise. People mattered—money didn't. Adventure mattered—comforts not so much. The world mattered—the pebble in her shoe she could ignore. Dreams mattered—the mundane took care of itself.

Millie died a peaceful death in Las Vegas, Nevada, on February 6, 2017—one hundred years, four months, and twenty-one days after her birth in Lansing, New York. Her ashes will be interred in Las Vegas. Irving's ashes have gone to the Big Island of Hawaii. But portions of both will be cast into Zion Canyon, a place they both loved. And another portion of each will be cast into Fall Creek so that they can meander through Beebe Lake on the Cornell campus, flow down Fall Creek Gorge, over the 150-foot waterfall, and spill into Cayuga Lake where six miles north near Salmon Creek in Myers, it all began.

Millie and Irving, in their own ways and together in the end, lived lives that mattered.

While Andre's ashes sit abundantly in a crypt in a wall in the garden of the Mission San Luis Rey in Oceanside, California, it is striking how much demand there is for Millie and Irving's limited ashes to spread to the places across the world where they had impact. There are life lessons here.

> Eventually, all things merge into one, and a river runs through
> it. The river was cut by the world's great flood and runs
> over rocks from the basement of time. On some of the rocks
> are timeless raindrops. Under the rocks are the words, and
> some of the words are theirs. I am haunted by waters.
> —Norman Maclean

Made in the USA
Monee, IL
12 September 2021